Developing Numeracy

CALCULATIONS

ACTIVITIES FOR THE DAILY MATHS LESSON

year

6

Dave Kirkby

A & C BLACK

Contents

Introduction 4

Understanding addition and subtraction

| The jester's hat | using mental methods to find an average (mean) | 6 |

Mental calculation strategies (+ and –)

Tombstones — finding a difference by counting up through the next multiple of 10, 100 or 1000 — 7

School numbers — identifying near doubles — 8

Tossing the welly! — adding or subtracting the nearest whole number — 9

TV ratings — adding or subtracting the nearest whole number — 10

Calculation genius — using the relationship between addition and subtraction — 11

Hexmonsters — adding three or more multiples of 10 — 12

Sports shop — adding several numbers by looking for pairs that make multiples of 10 — 13

Totals — adding several numbers by multiplying by a chosen number — 14

London sights — adding or subtracting a pair of four-digit multiples of 100 — 15

Apples and pears — adding or subtracting a pair of four-digit multiples of 100 — 16

Growing up — adding to a two-place decimal number to make the next whole number — 17

Up and away! — adding to a decimal number to make the next whole number or tenth — 18

Shoals of fish — adding/subtracting pairs of decimal numbers — 19

Pencil and paper procedures (+ and –)

Fan count — developing informal methods of addition — 20

Eight-card trick — developing standard methods of addition — 21

Second-hand sale — developing standard methods of addition (different numbers of digits) — 22

Running backwards race — developing standard methods of addition (decimals with different numbers of digits) — 23

Counting up — developing informal methods of subtraction — 24

Dicing with subtraction — developing standard methods of subtraction — 25

Six-card shuffle — developing standard methods of subtraction (decimals) — 26

Understanding multiplication and division

Caterpillar calculations — using brackets — 27

Alien remainders — giving a quotient as a fraction — 28

Division cards — relating division and fractions — 29

Order! Order! — giving a quotient as a decimal — 30

Rapid recall of multiplication and division facts

Poultry products — knowing by heart multiplication facts up to 10 x 10 — 31

Division challenge — knowing by heart multiplication facts up to 10 x 10, and deriving corresponding division facts — 32

Extra-terrestrial triangles — knowing by heart multiplication facts up to 10 x 10, and deriving corresponding division facts — 33

Problems, problems! — knowing by heart the squares of numbers 1 to 10 — 34

Fabric squares — deriving squares of multiples of 10 to 100 — 35

Cut the ribbon	recalling doubles of decimals to two decimal places, and corresponding halves	36
Double or nothing	recalling doubles of all numbers up to 100	37
Shoe shops	knowing by heart or deriving rapidly doubles of multiples of 10 up to 1000, and corresponding halves	38
Maths Mega-brain Quiz	recalling doubles of multiples of 100 up to 10 000, and corresponding halves	39

Mental calculation strategies (x and ÷)

Doubling and halving machine	multiplying by doubling one number and halving the other	40
Cross-country race	multiplying by 15 by multiplying by 10, halving the result, then adding the two parts	41
Match tickets	multiplying by 50 or 25 by multiplying by 100, then dividing by 2 or 4	42
Multiplication tables	doubling, then doubling again to find x24 facts from x6 facts	43
Night out	working out multiplications using doubled facts	44
Martian multiplication	working out an unknown table from combinations of other known tables	45
101 Dalmatians	multiplying by 99 or 101 by multiplying by 100 then adjusting	46
Packets of paperclips	multiplying by 49 or 51 by multiplying by 50 then adjusting	47
a, b or c?	partitioning and using the distributive law	48
Formula One digits	partitioning and using the distributive law	49
Four facts	using the relationship between multiplication and division	50
Number Cruncher	multiplying a decimal fraction by 10 or 100	51
Divine divisions	dividing a one- or two-digit whole number by 10 or 100	52
Parachute game	multiplying a decimal fraction by a single digit	53

Pencil and paper procedures (x and ÷)

Grid multiplication	developing informal methods of multiplication	54
More grid multiplication	developing informal methods of multiplication	55
Brains versus calculators!	developing standard methods of multiplication	56
Long multiplication	developing standard methods of multiplication (long multiplication)	57
Estimating and multiplying	developing standard methods of multiplication (decimals)	58
Sports Day	developing standard methods of division (long division)	59
Checking divisions	checking calculations, using the inverse operation	60
Odd-Bod or Even-Steven?	using knowledge of sums, differences or products of odd or even numbers	61

Answers

62–64

Reprinted 2002
Published 2002 by A & C Black Publishers Limited
37 Soho Square, London W1D 3QZ
www.acblack.com

ISBN 0-7136-6057-0

Copyright text © Dave Kirkby, 2002
Copyright illustrations © Michael Evans, 2002
Copyright cover illustration © Charlotte Hard, 2002
Editors: Lynne Williamson and Marie Lister

The author and publishers would like to thank Madeleine Madden and Corinne McCrum for their advice in producing this series of books.

A CIP catalogue record for this book is available from the British Library.

A & C Black uses paper produced with elemental chlorine-free pulp, harvested from managed sustainable forests.
Printed in Great Britain by Caligraving Ltd, Thetford, Norfolk.

Introduction

Developing Numeracy: Calculations is a series of seven photocopiable activity books designed to be used during the daily maths lesson. They focus on the second strand of the National Numeracy Strategy *Framework for teaching mathematics*. The activities are intended to be used in the time allocated to pupil activities; they aim to reinforce the knowledge, understanding and skills taught during the main part of the lesson and to provide practice and consolidation of the objectives contained in the framework document.

Year 6 supports the teaching of mathematics by providing a series of activities which develop important calculation skills. On the whole the activities are designed for children to work on independently, although this is not always possible and occasionally some children may need support.

Year 6 encourages children to:

- use known number facts and place value to consolidate mental addition and subtraction;
- use informal written methods for ThHTU +/– ThHTU;
- use standard written methods for ThHTU +/– ThHTU, addition of more than two such numbers, and addition/subtraction of decimal numbers (with either one or two decimal places);
- know by heart all multiplication facts up to 10 x 10;
- derive division facts from multiplication facts;
- begin to express a quotient as a fraction or as a decimal rounded to one decimal place;
- derive doubles of two-digit numbers (whole numbers or decimal numbers), multiples of 10 to 1000, multiples of 100 to 10000; and all corresponding halves;
- derive squares of multiples of 10 to 100;
- use known number facts and place value to consolidate mental multiplication and division;
- use standard written methods for short multiplication of ThHTU x U, U.th x U;
- use standard written methods for long multiplication of HTU x TU;
- use standard written methods for short division of decimals (TU.t ÷ U) and long division (HTU ÷ TU).

Extension

Many of the activity sheets end with a challenge (**Now try this!**) which reinforces and extends the children's learning, and provides the teacher with the opportunity for assessment. On occasion it may be necessary to read the instructions with the children before they begin the activity. For some of the challenges the children will need to record their answers on a separate piece of paper.

Organisation

Very little equipment is needed, but it will be useful to have available: coloured pencils, counters, scissors, calculators, dice and timers. Children may need number lines, 1–100 number squares and multiplication squares. These can be used to model mental calculations, but encourage the children to calculate without using them wherever possible.

Other useful counting equipment includes interlocking cubes, base ten material, place-value boards, and number cards. Ideally a variety of different types of apparatus should be used to help children understand concepts and develop mathematical language.

The activities in this book will naturally bring in elements of counting and problem solving. Children need to be confident and efficient in counting to be able to develop their calculation skills effectively. They will need regular counting practice to consolidate and develop the skills outlined in the Numbers and the Number System strand of the Strategy for Year 6 (see **Developing Numeracy: Numbers and the Number System Year 6**).

To help teachers select appropriate learning experiences for the children, the activities are grouped into sections within this book. However, the activities are not expected to be used in that order; the sheets are intended to support, rather than direct, the teacher's planning. Some activities are deliberately more challenging than others, to allow for the widely varying ability in most classrooms. Many activities can be made easier or more challenging by masking and substituting some of the numbers. You may wish to re-use some pages by copying them onto card and laminating them, or by enlarging them onto A3 paper.

Teachers' notes

Brief notes are provided at the foot of each page giving ideas and suggestions for maximising the effectiveness of the activity sheets. These can be masked before copying.

Notes on calculation methods

Multiplication

Common practice is to describe the x sign as 'lots of' or 'groups of' (which younger children find easier to understand), rather than the more precise 'multiplied by'. This 'lots of' approach has the effect of reversing the repeated addition, for example 3 multiplied by 4 (3 + 3 + 3 + 3) becomes 3 lots of 4 (4 + 4 + 4). The critical thing is to teach children that the order of multiplication does not matter, i.e. 3 x 4 = 4 x 3. If this is done, it matters less which method is taught.

A school needs to decide whether to initially teach multiplication using 'lots of' to describe the x sign or the slightly more mathematical 'multiplied by'.

Throughout this series, multiplication is treated as 'lots of' for continuity.

Checking results
Calculators are a valuable and essential aid in developing calculation skills and can be used to provide immediate feedback to children as to whether or not a particular calculation is correct.

Children should be encouraged to use other checking procedures besides calculators. Many activities allow for checking by using an inverse operation, for example using division to check a multiplication. This reinforces the links between adding and subtracting, multiplying and dividing, doubling and halving.

Estimation
Encourage the children to acquire the habit of making an estimate before attempting any calculation which cannot be done mentally. This develops rounding skills and gives a sense of the size of the answer. Encourage children always to follow up the calculation by comparing the answer with the estimate.

Recording written calculations
When children are working on written calculations, it is likely that they will be working at different levels. Some may still be using informal methods, whereas others may be ready for more sophisticated methods. It is recommended that the sheets be used flexibly, and adapted to suit the methods appropriate for individual children.

Whole-class warm-up activities
The following activities provide some practical ideas which can be used to introduce the main teaching part of the lesson.

Rapid recall of number facts

Sliding box
Make strips of card, all the same size, each showing a different number fact (for example, make a set of cards showing x7 multiplication facts). Make a sliding 'box' by cutting parallel slots in a rectangular piece of card, as shown.

 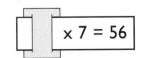

Slide the box to different positions on the strips and ask the children to say the hidden number.

Flash cards
Make sets of cards, each showing a number fact on the front and the answer on the reverse, for example, squares of numbers 1 to 12. The children can use these to practise recalling facts, then turn them over to check the answer.

front reverse

Double-sided practice cards
Make sets of cards to practise doubling and halving skills. For example, for the doubles of two-digit decimal numbers, write some decimal numbers in red on one side of the cards, and their corresponding doubles in blue on the other side. Shuffle the cards and arrange them with the red numbers face up to provide a set of random doubling tasks. The children can check the answers by looking at the reverse side. Then place the blue numbers face up to provide halving practice.

Similar sets of cards can be produced for other facts, for example 'multiplying by 7' and 'dividing by 7'.

Multiplication square
A multiplication square can be used to check the first ten multiples of any number. Give the children plenty of practice in chanting the multiples of numbers from 2 to 10. Chant the multiples, both forwards and backwards, first with the multiplication square and then without.

Mental calculation strategies

1–100 square
A 1–100 square provides a model for mental addition and subtraction involving two-digit numbers. Moving down a column illustrates adding tens, and moving up illustrates subtracting tens. Sliding right illustrates adding ones, and sliding left illustrates subtracting ones.

Number lines
Unlabelled 10-point and 100-point number lines are valuable resources for modelling mental addition and subtraction skills. Label the ends of the line with numbers appropriate to the calculation. Addition can be modelled by jumping from left to right along the line (i.e. counting on), and subtraction by jumping from right to left along the line (i.e. counting back). Number lines are also useful for encouraging awareness of the positional sense of numbers, for example two-place decimal numbers from 0 to 1.

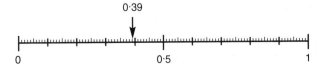

The jester's hat

The numbers on the jester's hat are consecutive .
Their total is on the jester's forehead.

- Write the consecutive numbers on the hats.

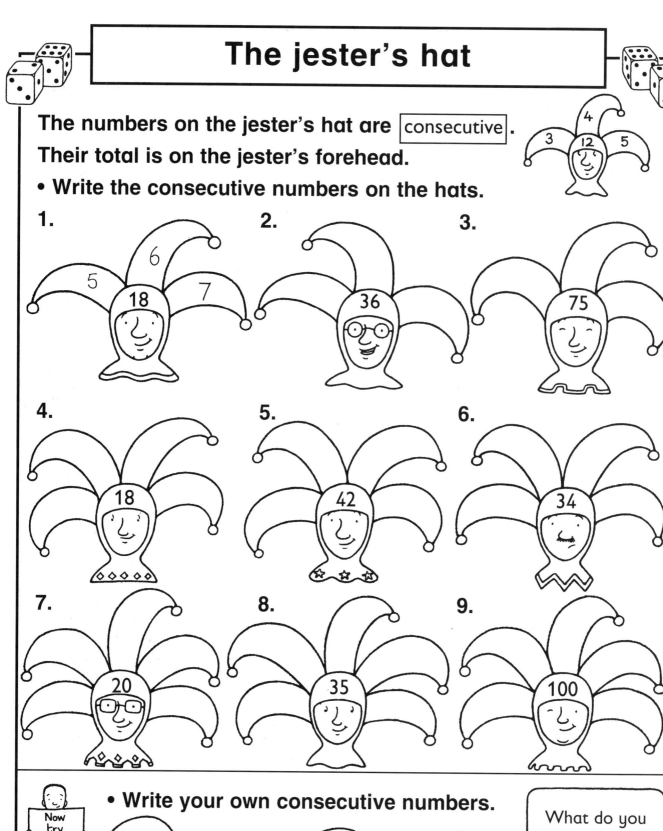

1.
5 6 7
18

2.
36

3.
75

4.
18

5.
42

6.
34

7.
20

8.
35

9.
100

- Write your own consecutive numbers.

Now try this!

What do you notice about the totals?

Teachers' note The totals on hats with three 'prongs' are multiples of three, and the totals on hats with five prongs are multiples of five. The mean of numbers on hats with four prongs is between the two centre numbers, for example the mean of 3, 4, 5, 6 is 4·5. Suggest that the children divide the total by the number of prongs to find the mean.

**Developing Numeracy
Calculations Year 6
© A & C Black**

Tombstones

- Write the age of these people when they died.

1. **Hugo Furst**
born 1864
died 1935
age ___71___

2. **Lucy Lastic**
born 1758
died 1813
age _____

3. **Isla White**
born 1835
died 1914
age _____

4. **Eileen Dover**
born 1685
died 1723
age _____

5. **Ben Dover**
born 1564
died 1638
age _____

6. **Joe King**
born 1469
died 1512
age _____

7. **Neil Downe**
born 1783
died 1856
age _____

8. **Justin Time**
born 1891
died 1945
age _____

9. **Teresa Green**
born 1889
died 1964
age _____

10. **Frank Furter**
born 948
died 1027
age _____

11. **Harry Carry**
born 1279
died 1316
age _____

12. **Andy Mann**
born 1758
died 1803
age _____

- Write the year these people were born.

Now try this!

Phil Macavity
born _____
died 1947
age 76

Cristal Chandelier
born _____
died 1978
age 83

Daisy Chane
born _____
died 1649
age 58

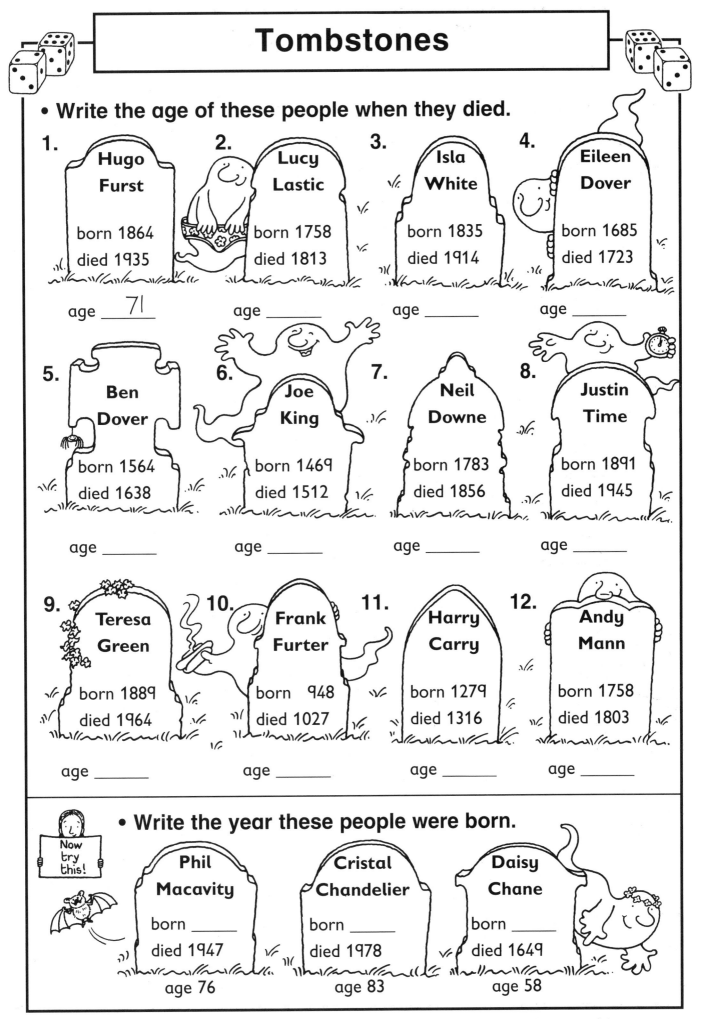

Teachers' note The children can draw a number line and show two jumps, one up to the next multiple of 1000 and one on to the larger number. They then add the two jumps together to find the difference.

Developing Numeracy Calculations Year 6 © A & C Black

School numbers

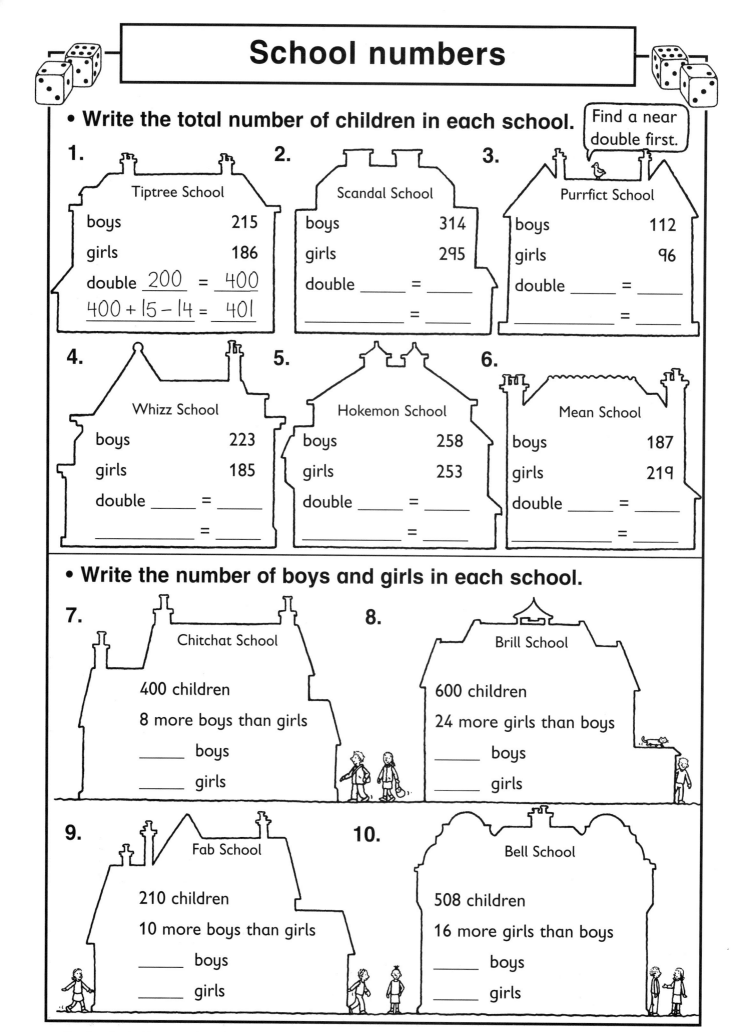

- **Write the total number of children in each school.**

> Find a near double first.

1. Tiptree School
boys 215
girls 186
double 200 = 400
400 + 15 - 14 = 401

2. Scandal School
boys 314
girls 295
double ____ = ____
____ = ____

3. Purrfict School
boys 112
girls 96
double ____ = ____
____ = ____

4. Whizz School
boys 223
girls 185
double ____ = ____
____ = ____

5. Hokemon School
boys 258
girls 253
double ____ = ____
____ = ____

6. Mean School
boys 187
girls 219
double ____ = ____
____ = ____

- **Write the number of boys and girls in each school.**

7. Chitchat School
400 children
8 more boys than girls
____ boys
____ girls

8. Brill School
600 children
24 more girls than boys
____ boys
____ girls

9. Fab School
210 children
10 more boys than girls
____ boys
____ girls

10. Bell School
508 children
16 more girls than boys
____ boys
____ girls

Teachers' note Encourage the children to calculate mentally, for example, when adding 215 and 186, point out that the numbers above/below 200 amount to one more than 400. Ask them to check their answers to the last four questions, as children often end up with double the required difference (in question 7, for example, by adding 8 to one half and subtracting 8 from the other, giving a difference of 16).

Developing Numeracy Calculations Year 6 © A & C Black

Tossing the welly!

Each contestant has two throws of the welly.

- **Write the distance of the best throw.**

> To add 2·9 you can add 3, then subtract 0·1.

1.

worst throw   7·5 m

improvement   1·9 m

best throw   _9·4_ m

2.

worst throw   12·6 m

improvement   2·9 m

best throw _____ m

3.

worst throw   14·3 m

improvement   3·9 m

best throw _____ m

4.

worst throw   9·6 m

improvement   2·8 m

best throw _____ m

5.

worst throw   7·3 m

improvement   3·1 m

best throw _____ m

6.

worst throw   15·7 m

improvement   4·8 m

best throw _____ m

- **Write the distance of the worst throw.**

7.

worst throw _____ m

improvement   1·9 m

best throw   8·6 m

8.

worst throw _____ m

improvement   2·9 m

best throw   11·7 m

9.

worst throw _____ m

improvement   3·8 m

best throw   14·3 m

10.

worst throw _____ m

improvement   4·1 m

best throw   15·6 m

11.

worst throw _____ m

improvement   0·9 m

best throw   7·8 m

12.

worst throw _____ m

improvement   1·8 m

best throw   10·4 m

> Now try this!

Sally has a best throw of 11·6 m . Her improvement is one-third of her worst throw.

- **What was her worst throw?** _____

Teachers' note The mathematics can be modelled on a 100-point number line, with the ends labelled 0 and 10. Encourage the children to check their answers using the inverse operation, for example in the second activity, adding the worst throw and the improvement to check that they total the best throw.

Developing Numeracy Calculations Year 6 © A & C Black

TV ratings

The number of people watching TV shows changes year by year. Some numbers increase and some decrease.

- **Write the new figures for each show.**

Quizbat!

last year	3·5 million
up	0·9 million
now	4·4 million

The Sampsons

last year	7·6 million
up	2·9 million
now	_____ million

Match of the Week

last year	8·5 million
down	1·9 million
now	_____ million

Who wants to be a Pauper?

last year	12·6 million
up	2·8 million
now	_____ million

Home and Alone

last year	4·6 million
down	0·9 million
now	_____ million

Next Door

last year	10·7 million
down	3·9 million
now	_____ million

- **Write the ratings for last year.**

Crown Street

last year	_____ million
up	1·9 million
now	12·3 million

West-enders

last year	_____ million
up	2·8 million
now	10·3 million

Bottom of the Pops

last year	_____ million
down	3·8 million
now	9·4 million

This year, Sampsons viewers have each given 1p to charity. Home and Alone viewers have each given 3p.
- **Who gave more, and by how much?** _____

_____

Teachers' note The mathematics can be modelled on a 100-point number line, with the ends labelled 0 and 10. As a further extension, ask the children to start with their answer and add/subtract the rise/fall in viewing figures to check that they get the original number. Encourage children to explain their strategy, for example to subtract 3·9, take away 4, then add 0·1 back on to the answer.

Developing Numeracy Calculations Year 6 © A & C Black

10

Calculation genius

• **Complete these four calculations.**

Check these answers on a calculator.

$1.36 + 2.47 =$ _____ $5.3 + 0.17 =$ _____

$4.62 - 1.3 \ =$ _____ $2.73 - 0.8 \ =$ _____

• **Use the calculations above to help you find these answers.**

1. $1.93 + 0.8 \ =$ _____

2. $5.47 - 0.17 =$ _____

3. $2.73 - 1.93 =$ _____

4. $3.32 + 1.3 \ =$ _____

5. $3.83 - 1.36 =$ _____

6. $5.47 - 5.3 \ =$ _____

7. $4.62 - 3.32 =$ _____

8. $3.83 - 2.47 =$ _____

• **Find these answers. Adjust the calculations in questions 1 to 8 to help you find the answers.**

9. $1.93 + 2.8 \ =$ _____

10. $5.47 - 3.3 \ =$ _____

11. $3.83 - 2.36 =$ _____

12. $3.32 + 4.3 \ =$ _____

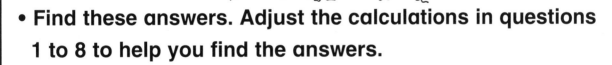

Now try this!

• **Write nine additions or subtractions. Use only these five numbers.** $1.72 \quad 5.93 \quad 4.21 \quad 2.49 \quad 6.7$

_____   _____   _____

_____   _____   _____

_____   _____   _____

Teachers' note The links between addition and subtraction will be better understood if the children are frequently asked to use a subtraction to check an addition, and an addition to check a subtraction.

Developing Numeracy Calculations Year 6 © A & C Black

Hexmonsters

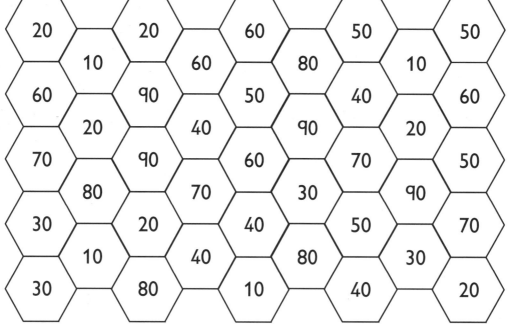

The number on the monster's head is the total of the numbers on its body.

• **Find each monster in the grid. Write the numbers on its body.**

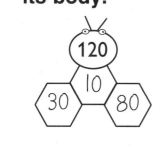

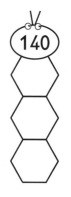

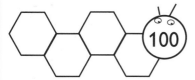

 • **Find monsters with totals of** 200 **and** 300 **.**

Teachers' note Encourage the children to make the link between adding multiples of 10, for example 50, 70 and 30, and adding single digits, such as 5, 7 and 3. There may be more than one solution for any monster.

**Developing Numeracy
Calculations Year 6
© A & C Black**

Sports shop

• Complete the totals.

Look for pairs that make multiples of 10, for example 23 and 37.

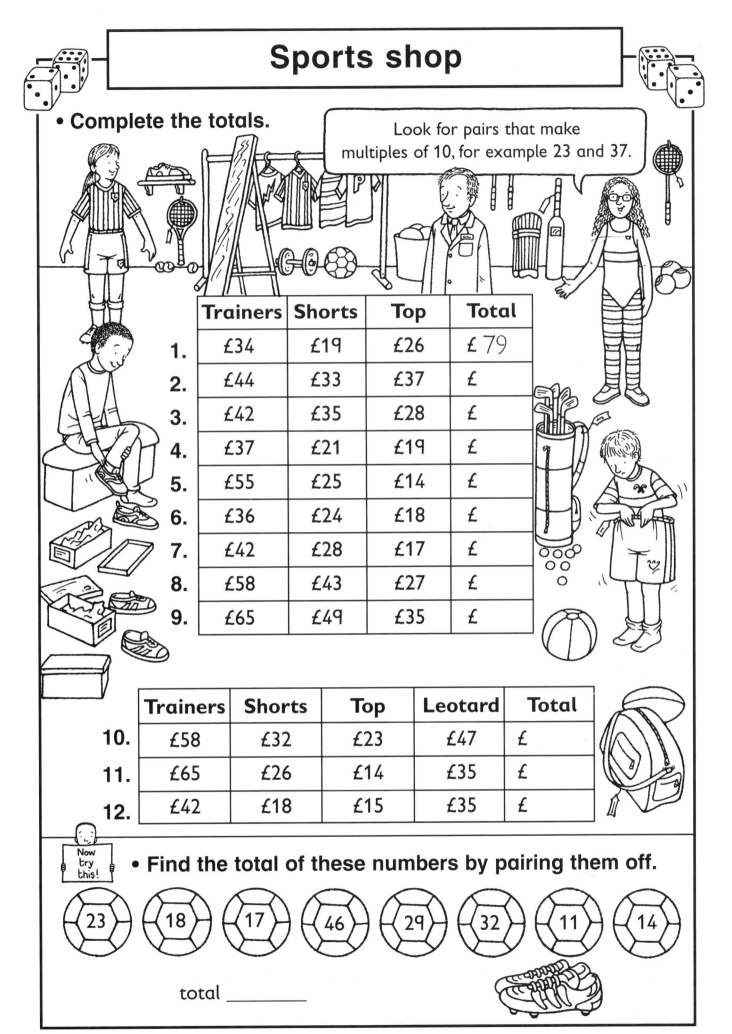

	Trainers	Shorts	Top	Total
1.	£34	£19	£26	£ 79
2.	£44	£33	£37	£
3.	£42	£35	£28	£
4.	£37	£21	£19	£
5.	£55	£25	£14	£
6.	£36	£24	£18	£
7.	£42	£28	£17	£
8.	£58	£43	£27	£
9.	£65	£49	£35	£

	Trainers	Shorts	Top	Leotard	Total
10.	£58	£32	£23	£47	£
11.	£65	£26	£14	£35	£
12.	£42	£18	£15	£35	£

Now try this!

• Find the total of these numbers by pairing them off.

23   18   17   46   29   32   11   14

total _____

Teachers' note When adding numbers of this kind, for example 34, 19 and 26, the children can add number pairs which make multiples of 10, i.e. 34 and 26 (60), then add the other number. Alternatively, they can start by adding the tens (60) and then add on the units, looking for pairs which make 10, i.e. (4 + 6) + 9.

Developing Numeracy
Calculations Year 6
© A & C Black

Totals

• **Write the total weight of each group.**

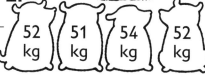

Use multiplying first.

1.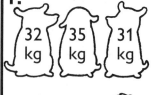

32 kg 35 kg 31 kg

$(3 \times 30) + 8$
$= 90 + 8$
$= 98 \text{ kg}$

2. 52 kg 51 kg 54 kg 52 kg _____

3. 82 kg 81 kg 83 kg _____

4. 65 kg 63 kg 62 kg 64 kg _____

• **Write the total of the ringed numbers in each row.**

1	2	③	④	⑤	⑥	7	8	9	10
11	⑫	13	⑭	15	⑯	17	18	⑲	20
21	22	㉓	24	㉕	26	㉗	28	29	30
㉛	㉜	33	34	㉟	㊱	37	38	39	40
41	42	㊸	㊹	45	46	㊼	48	49	50
�51	�52	㊳	㊴	㊵	56	57	58	59	60
61	62	㊿	㊿	65	66	㊻	68	69	70
㋄	㋅	73	74	㋕	㋖	77	78	79	80
81	82	㋝	㋞	㋟	86	㋡	㋢	89	90
㋩	92	㋫	㋬	95	㋮	97	98	㋯	100

$3 + 4 + 5 + 6$ = _____

_____ = _____

_____ = _____

_____ = _____

_____ = _____

_____ = _____

_____ = _____

_____ = _____

_____ = _____

_____ = _____

Now try this!

• **Write:**

three numbers that total 158 _____

four numbers that total 127 _____

five numbers that total 265 _____

six numbers that total 444 _____

Teachers' note In the extension activity, ensure that the children use a similar strategy to that used in the main activity, and start by dividing the total approximately by the number of numbers.

Developing Numeracy
Calculations Year 6
© A & C Black

London sights

The chart shows the number of visitors to London's major attractions.

* Complete the chart.

Name of attraction	British visitors	Foreign visitors	Total
Tower of London	2 300	5 600	7 900
Madame Tussauds	2 700	6 400	
Houses of Parliament	1 900	6 500	
Trafalgar Square	1 700	7 300	
London Zoo	2 800	3 900	
London Aquarium	4 700	7 400	
London Planetarium	2 600		7 300
Buckingham Palace	3 800		9 700
Natural History Museum	4 900		8 600
Downing Street	1 800		6 400
The London Eye	2 300		7 200
St Paul's Cathedral	3 200		6 100

Last month the number of foreign visitors was twice the number of British visitors.

* Complete the chart.

British visitors	Foreign visitors	Total
		8 100
		9 300
		12 600

Now try this!

**Developing Numeracy
Calculations Year 6
© A & C Black**

15

Apples and pears

• **Play this game with a partner.**

☆ Shuffle each set of number cards, keeping the sets separate.

☆ Place them face down in two piles: LEFT and RIGHT.

☆ Take turns to reveal a card from each pile.

☆ Find the matching numbers on the leaves.

☆ Add the numbers on the apple and the pear.

☆ If your partner agrees with the answer, score one point for each thousand in the answer. **Example**: 8200 scores 8 points.

☆ The winner is the first to reach **50** points.

You need two sets of number cards 1 to 10.

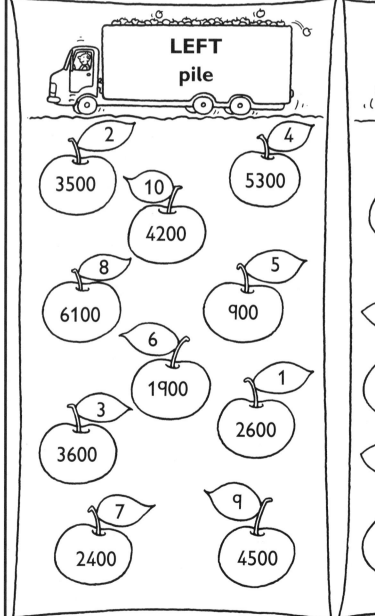

LEFT pile

leaf	value
2	3500
4	5300
10	4200
8	6100
5	900
6	1900
1	2600
3	3600
7	2400
9	4500

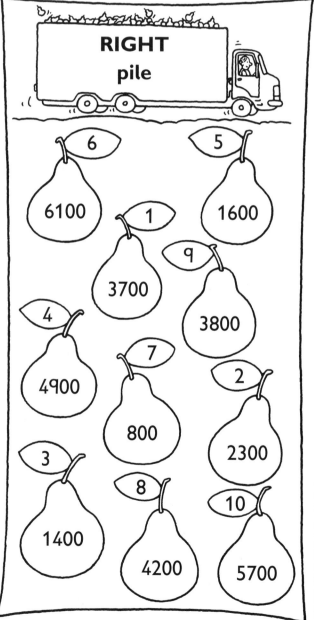

RIGHT pile

leaf	value
6	6100
5	1600
1	3700
9	3800
4	4900
7	800
2	2300
3	1400
8	4200
10	5700

Teachers' note Help the children to recognise that the calculations are equivalent to adding two-digit numbers. An alternative game is to find the difference between the two numbers (the winner is the first to reach 15 points).

Developing Numeracy Calculations Year 6 © A & C Black

Growing up

- **Write how much taller each dinosaur must grow to reach the next whole metre.**

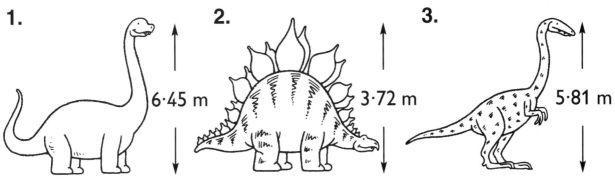

1. 6·45 m

_0·55_ m to grow

2. 3·72 m

_____ m to grow

3. 5·81 m

_____ m to grow

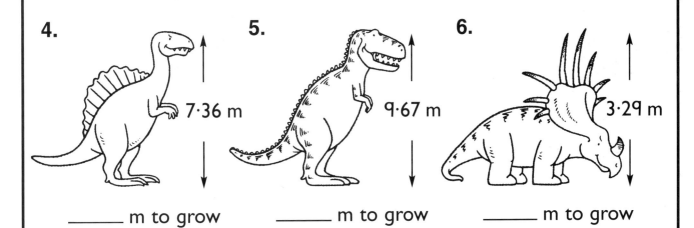

4. 7·36 m

_____ m to grow

5. 9·67 m

_____ m to grow

6. 3·29 m

_____ m to grow

- **What was the height of these dinosaurs?**

7.

Grew 0·32 m to reach 5 m. Was _____ m

8.

Grew 0·72 m to reach 9 m. Was _____ m

9.

Grew 0·08 m to reach 4 m. Was _____ m

Now try this!

A dinosaur was 1·55 m tall. It grew 33 cm each year for four years.

- **How much taller must it now grow to reach the next whole metre?** _____ m

---

Teachers' note Help the children to recognise that the skills involved are the same as for finding pairs of two-digit numbers which total 100.

**Developing Numeracy
Calculations Year 6
© A & C Black**

Up and away!

- **Join the balloons to the number lines.**
- **Complete the number sentences to make the next** `tenth` **and the next** `whole number` .

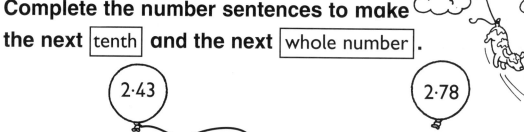

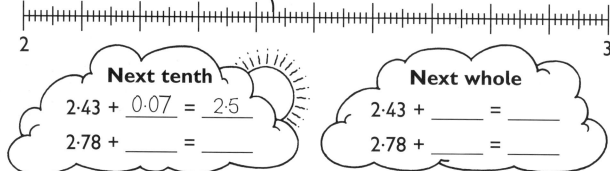

Next tenth

$2.43 + \underline{0.07} = \underline{2.5}$

$2.78 + \underline{} = \underline{}$

Next whole

$2.43 + \underline{} = \underline{}$

$2.78 + \underline{} = \underline{}$

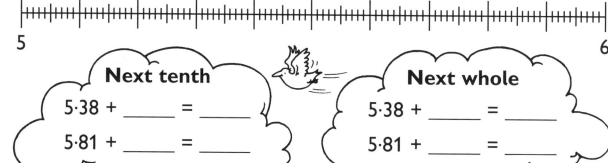

Next tenth

$5.38 + \underline{} = \underline{}$

$5.81 + \underline{} = \underline{}$

Next whole

$5.38 + \underline{} = \underline{}$

$5.81 + \underline{} = \underline{}$

- **Complete these number sentences.**

1. $5.63 + \underline{} = 6$

2. $4.27 + \underline{} = 5$

3. $3.87 + \underline{} = 3.9$

4. $4.16 + \underline{} = 4.2$

5. $7 - \underline{} = 6.47$

6. $8 - \underline{} = 7.08$

7. $4.6 - \underline{} = 4.54$

8. $1.9 - \underline{} = 1.83$

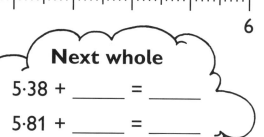

- **Check questions 1 to 4 using subtraction.**
- **Check questions 5 to 8 using addition.**

Use me!

Teachers' note The number lines will help the children to see the difference between adding to the next tenth and adding to the next whole number. It may help some children to count together along the number line in hundredths. Remind them that they are counting in jumps of 0.01.

**Developing Numeracy
Calculations Year 6
© A & C Black**

18

Shoals of fish

The number on a fish is the
total of the two fishes below it.

• Fill in the missing numbers.

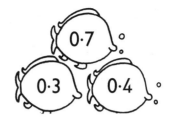

0.7

0.3   0.4

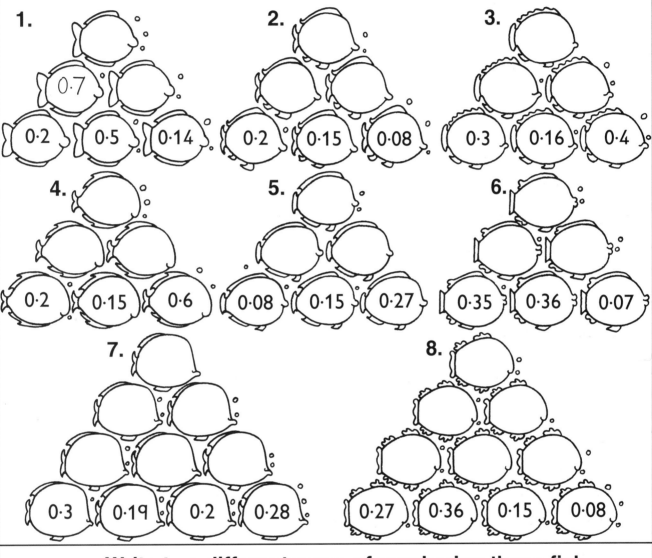

1.

0·7

0·2   0·5   0·14

2.

0·2   0·15   0·08

3.

0·3   0·16   0·4

4.

0·2   0·15   0·6

5.

0·08   0·15   0·27

6.

0·35   0·36   0·07

7.

0·3   0·19   0·2   0·28

8.

0·27   0·36   0·15   0·08

• Write two different ways of numbering these fish.

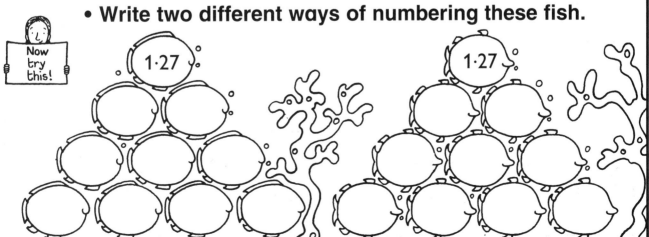

Now try this!

1·27

1·27

Teachers' note As a further extension, give the children some blank shoals of fish so that they can
choose their own bottom numbers. Extend to shoals which have five fish on the bottom.

Developing Numeracy
Calculations Year 6
© A & C Black

Fan count

- **Find the total number of fans at each ice-hockey match.**

1.

Panthers v Cheetahs

| 4378 | | 2156 |

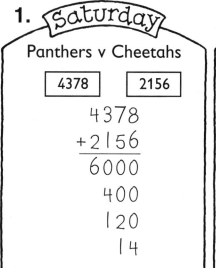

```
  4378
+ 2156
  6000
   400
   120
    14
```

[____] fans

2. Saturday

Tigers v Lions

| 1769 | | 1835 |

[____] fans

You could first add the thousands, then add the hundreds, then the tens, then the units.

Show your workings.

3. Sunday

Penguins v Ice Bears

| 2146 | | 1974 |

[____] fans

4. Sunday

Seals v Sealions

| 2777 | | 1835 |

[____] fans

5. Sunday

Wolves v Whales

| 4621 | | 1094 |

[____] fans

- **Find the total number of fans on Saturday. Then find the total on Sunday.**

Saturday

Sunday

Teachers' note Invite the children to estimate each total before they start, writing their estimates on another sheet of paper. They can estimate by rounding each number to its nearest thousand before adding. The space for working out has been left blank to allow children to record in their most familiar way.

**Developing Numeracy
Calculations Year 6
© A & C Black**

Eight-card trick

- **Find which number cards make these totals. You can use a number only once in each calculation.**

1.

3	5	8	4
+ 2	6	1	7

6	2	0	1
	1	1	1

2.

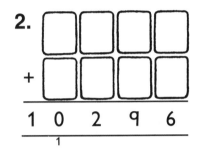

1	0	2	9	6
		1		

3.

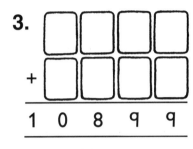

1	0	8	9	9

4.

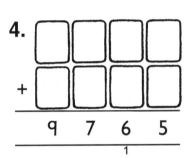

9	7	6	5
		1	

5.

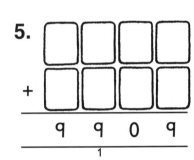

9	9	0	9
		1	

6.

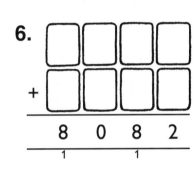

8	0	8	2
	1		1

7.

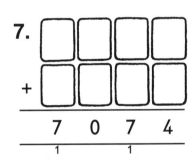

7	0	7	4
	1		1

8.

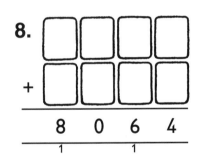

8	0	6	4
		1	1

9.

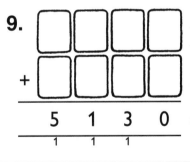

5	1	3	0
	1	1	1

- **Use the cards to make the largest possible total and the smallest possible total.**

largest _____ smallest _____

Teachers' note The children should use a set of number cards 1 to 8 and explore arrangements, trying to make the given total. When they have succeeded, they can then write in the numbers on the sheet.

Developing Numeracy Calculations Year 6 © A & C Black

Second-hand sale

a	b	c	d	e	f

£7543	£1257	£791	£463	£48	£8

- **Estimate the total cost. Then calculate the actual cost.**
- **Show your workings in the space.**

1. a + b

estimate

£

actual

£

2. d + e

estimate

£

actual

£

3. f + c

estimate

£

actual

£

4. a + b + c

estimate

£

actual

£

5. c + d + e

estimate

£

actual

£

6. e + f + a

estimate

£

actual

£

7. a + b + d + e

estimate

£

actual

£

8. c + b + f + d

estimate

£

actual

£

9. f + e + d + a

estimate

£

actual

£

Teachers' note Stress the importance of ensuring that numbers set out below one another should have digits aligned in their correct columns. The space for working out has been left blank to allow the children to record in their own way.

**Developing Numeracy
Calculations Year 6
© A & C Black**

Running backwards race

These are the finishing times for the running backwards race.

Dice roll	1	2	3	4	5	6
Finishing time	7·25 sec	4·8 sec	124·9 sec	16 sec	29·7 sec	0·34 sec

• **Play this game with a partner.**

☆ Roll the dice three times. Write down the matching finishing times. Do this for all six calculations.

☆ Estimate the total time for each calculation.

☆ Swap sheets and add up your partner's calculations.

☆ The winner is the player whose estimates are closer.

> **You each need** a dice and a copy of this sheet.

estimate _____

\+

estimate _____

\+

estimate _____

\+

estimate _____

\+

estimate _____

\+

estimate _____

\+

Now try this!

• **Choose three numbers to make a total close to the estimate.**

28·6	9·3	4·08
7	13·2	0·9

estimate 40

\+

estimate 20

\+

estimate 25

\+

Teachers' note Stress the importance of ensuring that the digits of each number appear in their correct column. Remind the children that 16, for example, is 16·00. When estimating, they will need to round the numbers to the nearest ten or whole number. To find whose estimates are closer, ask them to find the difference between their estimate and the actual total, and total this for all six calculations.

Developing Numeracy Calculations Year 6 © A & C Black

Counting up

- **Complete these subtractions by counting up from the smaller number to the larger. Estimate first.**

1. estimate <u>3000</u>

```
  5 3 5 6
- 2 4 8 7
```
.... 1 3 (2500)
.... 5 0 0 (3000)
.... 2 3 5 6 (5356)
_____
.... 2 8 6 9

2. estimate _____

```
  5 8 3 2
- 2 1 7 4
```
.... (   )
.... (   )
.... (   )
_____

3. estimate _____

```
  4 6 1 5
- 3 2 7 9
```
.... (   )
.... (   )
.... (   )
_____

4. estimate _____

```
  8 3 5 1
- 2 6 7 6
```
.... (   )
.... (   )
.... (   )
_____

5. estimate _____

```
  7 1 4 0
- 2 8 3 8
```
.... (   )
.... (   )
.... (   )
_____

6. estimate _____

```
  7 5 2 8
- 6 3 3 9
```
.... (   )
.... (   )
.... (   )
_____

Now try this!

- **For questions 1, 2 and 3, subtract the answer from the top number. What do you notice?**

estimate _____

```
  5 3 5 6
- 2 8 6 9
```
.... (   )
.... (   )
.... (   )
_____

estimate _____

```
  5 8 3 2
-
```
_____
.... (   )
.... (   )
.... (   )
_____

estimate _____

```
  4 6 1 5
-
```
_____
.... (   )
.... (   )
.... (   )
_____

Teachers' note Estimates can be made by rounding each number to its nearest thousand. The extension activity illustrates how we can check answers by doing the inverse operation.

**Developing Numeracy
Calculations Year 6**
© A & C Black

Dicing with subtraction

• **Play this game with a partner.**

☆ Each player rolls a dice.
☆ Write the dice number in any space on your board.
☆ Continue to roll the dice until all the spaces are filled for Round 1.
☆ Calculate your answers.
☆ The winner of a round is the player with the largest total.

You need a dice each.

Remember, the larger number needs to be at the top when you subtract.

Name	Name

Round 1

☐☐ ☐☐
− ☐☐ ☐☐
☐

☐☐ ☐☐
− ☐☐ ☐☐
☐

Round 2

☐☐ ☐
− ☐☐ ☐
☐

☐☐ ☐
− ☐☐ ☐
☐

Round 3

☐☐ ☐☐
− ☐☐ ☐☐
☐

☐☐ ☐☐
− ☐☐ ☐☐
☐

Teachers' note Encourage the children to think carefully about where to place the dice numbers to give them the greatest chance of winning. A variation on the game is to aim for the smallest total, or the total nearest to 3000. Children who wish to use a different subtraction strategy can use the back of the worksheet to show their workings before filling in the answer.

Developing Numeracy Calculations Year 6 © A & C Black

Six-card shuffle

- **Use number cards 3 to 8.**

  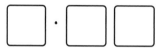

3	4	5	6	7	8

- **Arrange them to make six different subtractions. Write the answers.**

Make sure that the top number is greater than the bottom number.

1.

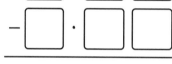

```
  ⁴5̶ . ¹6  8
-  3 . 7  4
─────────────
   1 . 9  4
```

2.

3.

4.

5.

6.

- **Now use number cards 5 to 9.**

5	6	7	8	9

- **Make subtractions. Write the answers.**

7.

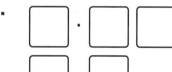

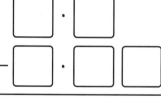

8.

9.

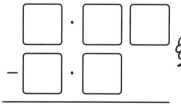

10.

Teachers' note Each child needs a set of number cards 3–9. When subtracting decimals with different numbers of decimal places, as in questions 7–10, the children will need to add some zeros. They could work together to make up the subtractions and then set a timer to compete against each other to complete the answers.

Developing Numeracy Calculations Year 6 © A & C Black

Caterpillar calculations

- **Use the digits on the caterpillar to make each target number. You can use each digit only once, but you do not have to use all four.**

1.

targets	
30 →	$(4 \times 5) + 3 + 7$
44 →	
24 →	
50 →	
58 →	

2.

targets	
19 →	
52 →	
36 →	
18 →	
25 →	

3.

targets	
26 →	
55 →	
36 →	
30 →	
54 →	

4.

targets	
26 →	
38 →	
18 →	
49 →	
50 →	

Now try this!

- **Use the digits** [1], [5], [7] **and** [4].
- **Make these targets, using brackets each time.**

targets	
21 →	
22 →	
23 →	
24 →	
25 →	

targets	
26 →	
27 →	
28 →	
29 →	
30 →	

Teachers' note Before beginning the activity, thoroughly revise the use of brackets to ensure that the children fully understand their use, for example, (4 x 5) + 3 + 7 should not be confused with 4 x (5 + 3) + 7. Some children may find this exercise difficult. As a variation, allow the children to create two-digit numbers, for example 44 = 54 − (7 + 3).

**Developing Numeracy
Calculations Year 6
© A & C Black**

- **Complete these remainder charts. Divide the number on the alien by the numbers ⟨2⟩ to ⟨10⟩. Write the remainder as a fraction, as simply as possible.**

1.

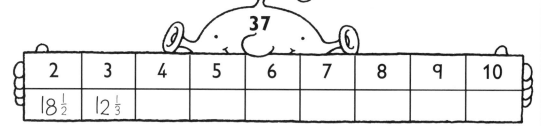

37

divide by

2	3	4	5	6	7	8	9	10
$18\frac{1}{2}$	$12\frac{1}{3}$							

2.

48

divide by

2	3	4	5	6	7	8	9	10

3.

80

divide by

2	3	4	5	6	7	8	9	10

4.

28

divide by

2	3	4	5	6	7	8	9	10

Now try this!

- **Complete a remainder chart for your own alien number.**

divide by

2	3	4	5	6	7	8	9	10

Teachers' note Encourage the children to simplify fractions such as $\frac{3}{6}$, for example, to $\frac{1}{2}$. For some numbers (such as prime numbers), each of the nine divisions has a remainder. Other numbers have many exact divisions with no remainders. Children can investigate which numbers, up to 100, have the greatest number of exact divisions.

Developing Numeracy Calculations Year 6 © A & C Black

Division cards

This game is for three players. One is the calculation checker.

☆ Cut out the cards. Spread them face down.

☆ Decide who will be the calculation checker.

☆ The other two players choose a card each and answer the division.
   Example: for 19 ÷ 6 say 'three and one-sixth'.

☆ The calculation checker checks that the answers are correct. The player with the largest answer keeps the cards.

☆ The winner is the player who collects the most cards.

☆ Play again, choosing a different player to be the checker.

Use a multiplication square to help you check.

$\dfrac{44}{5}$	$\dfrac{1}{7}$ of 15	22 ÷ 5	$\dfrac{34}{6}$
39 ÷ 7	$\dfrac{1}{4}$ of 13	$\dfrac{24}{7}$	$\dfrac{1}{6}$ of 27
$\dfrac{16}{5}$	$\dfrac{1}{7}$ of 50	$\dfrac{21}{4}$	$\dfrac{23}{8}$
25 ÷ 8	19 ÷ 6	$\dfrac{1}{8}$ of 43	$\dfrac{1}{5}$ of 37
27 ÷ 4	$\dfrac{59}{8}$	$\dfrac{1}{4}$ of 35	46 ÷ 6

Teachers' note You could photocopy the sheet onto card before cutting. Provide multiplication squares to help the children check the answers. A variation of the game is that the player with the smallest answer (or nearest to 6) keeps the cards.

**Developing Numeracy
Calculations Year 6
© A & C Black**

Order! Order!

- **Estimate** the order for each set of divisions. Use the letters **a** to **e**.

> Estimate from lowest answer to highest.

- **Complete the divisions. Write the remainder as a decimal.**

- **Write the actual order of the answers.**

	a	b	c	d	e		
1.	612 ÷ 100	60 ÷ 10	31 ÷ 5	13 ÷ 2	25 ÷ 4	est.	c d b a e
	6·12					act.	
2.	476 ÷ 100	49 ÷ 10	26 ÷ 5	11 ÷ 2	19 ÷ 4	est.	
						act.	
3.	212 ÷ 100	21 ÷ 10	13 ÷ 5	5 ÷ 2	9 ÷ 4	est.	
						act.	
4.	698 ÷ 100	70 ÷ 10	34 ÷ 5	15 ÷ 2	27 ÷ 4	est.	
						act.	
5.	910 ÷ 100	89 ÷ 10	46 ÷ 5	17 ÷ 2	35 ÷ 4	est.	
						act.	
6.	392 ÷ 100	39 ÷ 10	19 ÷ 5	8 ÷ 2	15 ÷ 4	est.	
						act.	

Now try this!

- **Write five different divisions. Each answer must be close to 7 and should have a decimal remainder.**

7|0 ÷ 100	_____ ÷ 10	_____ ÷ 5	_____ ÷ 2	_____ ÷ 4
= 7·1	=	=	=	=

Teachers' note The children should divide the numbers, expressing the answer as a fraction, and then convert the fraction to a decimal. It is difficult to compare the size of fractions, whereas it is easier to compare decimals. Hundredths and tenths are the simplest. Revise how to find the decimal equivalent of halves, quarters and fifths.

**Developing Numeracy
Calculations Year 6
© A & C Black**

Poultry products

- **Fill in the boxes.**

- **Use only the numbers** ☐1 **to** ☐10 .

1. ☐6 × ☐7 = ⬭42   **2.** ☐ × ☐ = ⬭63

3. ☐ × ☐ = ⬭27   **4.** ☐ × ☐ = ⬭54

5. ☐ × ☐ = ⬭8   **6.** ☐ × ☐ = ⬭80

There are ☐42 possible products, when multiplying
the numbers ☐1 to ☐10 .

- **Write them in order on the eggs. Use the**
  multiplication square to help you.

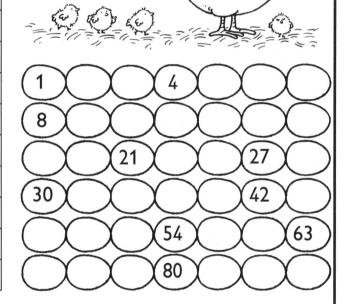

1	2	3	4	5	6	7	8	9	10
2	4	6	8	10	12	14	16	18	20
3	6	9	12	15	18	21	24	27	30
4	8	12	16	20	24	28	32	36	40
5	10	15	20	25	30	35	40	45	50
6	12	18	24	30	36	42	48	54	60
7	14	21	28	35	42	49	56	63	70
8	16	24	32	40	48	56	64	72	80
9	18	27	36	45	54	63	72	81	90
10	20	30	40	50	60	70	80	90	100

Eggs: 1, ⬭, ⬭, 4, ⬭, ⬭, ⬭, ⬭;
8, ⬭, ⬭, ⬭, ⬭, ⬭, ⬭, ⬭;
⬭, ⬭, 21, ⬭, ⬭, 27;
30, ⬭, ⬭, ⬭, 42;
⬭, ⬭, ⬭, 54, ⬭, 63;
⬭, ⬭, ⬭, 80, ⬭, ⬭

Now try this!

- **Find the** ☐13 **products which you can make in more**
  than one way.

  Example: ⬭6 = 1 × 6
              = 2 × 3

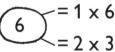
Remember, use only
numbers **1** to **10**.

Teachers' note The children could work in pairs for this activity. For the extension activity, explain
that 1 x 6 and 6 x 1 are treated as the same calculation for this exercise.

Developing Numeracy
Calculations Year 6
© A & C Black

Division challenge

If you follow these rules you can make 16 **different divisions.**
- **Try to find all 16!**

Work in a systematic way.

Use the digits **1** to **9** to make the divisions.
You may use a digit only **once** in each division.
You may use the same set of digits only once,
so you may include only one of these:

1 2 ÷ 4 = 3 or 1 2 ÷ 3 = 4

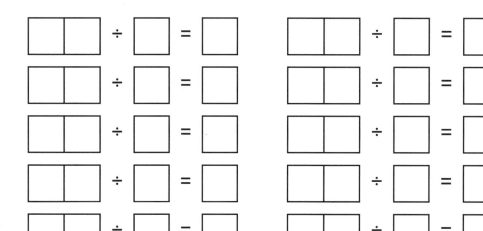

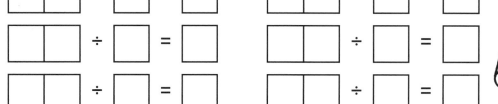

- **Make two different divisions.**

☐☐ ÷ ☐ = ☐☐

☐☐ ÷ ☐ = ☐☐

You must still follow the rules!

Teachers' note The children could work in pairs. They should experiment with number cards and work systematically, for example, looking for divisions dividing by 9, then by 8, etc. If the digit zero is allowed, then four more divisions are possible. In the extension activity, point out that the divisions should have a two-digit answer, for example 72 ÷ 4 = 18.

Developing Numeracy
Calculations Year 6
© A & C Black

Extra-terrestrial triangles

The number on a star is the [product] of the numbers either side of it.

Example: (5) — ◇40 — (8)

Top right triangle:
(4), ✦24, ✦12, (6), ✦18, (3)

• **Write the missing numbers.**

1. (4), (8) ✦ (3)

2. (7), (8) ✦ (6)

3. ✦24, (4) ✦36

• **Make up your own triangles.**

4.

5.

6.

• **Find the missing numbers.**

7. ✦56, ✦63, ✦72

8. ✦40, ✦20, ✦32

9. ✦27, ✦54, ✦18

Now try this!

Teachers' note The top row of triangles can be solved by deduction using the clues given. For the
extension activity, suggest to the children that they try a number in a circle which they know to be a
factor of the two star numbers either side, and see whether this leads to a solution.

Developing Numeracy
Calculations Year 6
© A & C Black

Problems, problems!

• **Follow the instructions to find the answer.**

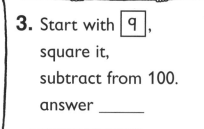

1. Start with ⟨7⟩,
square it,
add 3.
answer _____

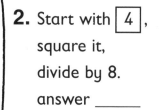

2. Start with ⟨4⟩,
square it,
divide by 8.
answer _____

3. Start with ⟨9⟩,
square it,
subtract from 100.
answer _____

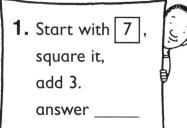

4. Start with ⟨5⟩,
multiply it by itself,
double it,
divide by 10.
answer _____

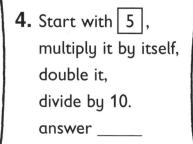

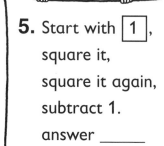

5. Start with ⟨1⟩,
square it,
square it again,
subtract 1.
answer _____

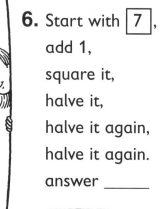

6. Start with ⟨7⟩,
add 1,
square it,
halve it,
halve it again,
halve it again.
answer _____

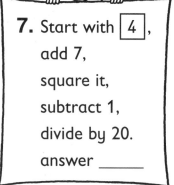

7. Start with ⟨4⟩,
add 7,
square it,
subtract 1,
divide by 20.
answer _____

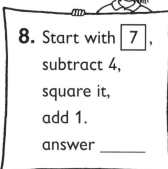

8. Start with ⟨7⟩,
subtract 4,
square it,
add 1.
answer _____

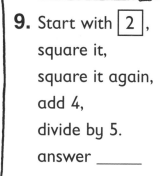

9. Start with ⟨2⟩,
square it,
square it again,
add 4,
divide by 5.
answer _____

• **Make up two problems for a partner to solve.**

Start with ☐,

Start with ☐,

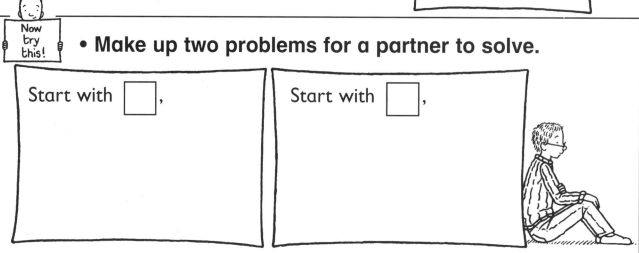

Teachers' note Challenge the children to do the calculations mentally. Children who find this difficult can write the number reached after each stage. Remind them that squaring is not the same as doubling.

**Developing Numeracy
Calculations Year 6
© A & C Black**

34

Fabric squares

• Write the ▢area of each square.   Example:

30 cm
area =
900 cm²
30 cm

1.   40 cm
area =
_____ cm²
40 cm

2.   70 cm
area =
_____ cm²
70 cm

3.   50 cm
area =
_____ cm²
50 cm

4.   60 cm
area =
_____ cm²
60 cm

5.   80 cm
area =
_____ cm²
80 cm

6.   90 cm
area =
_____ cm²
90 cm

7.   100 cm
area =
_____ cm²
100 cm

Now try this!

• If ▢100 cm² of fabric costs ▢£2.50, write the cost of a square which is:

100 cm x 100 cm   40 cm x 40 cm   80 cm x 80 cm

£   £   £

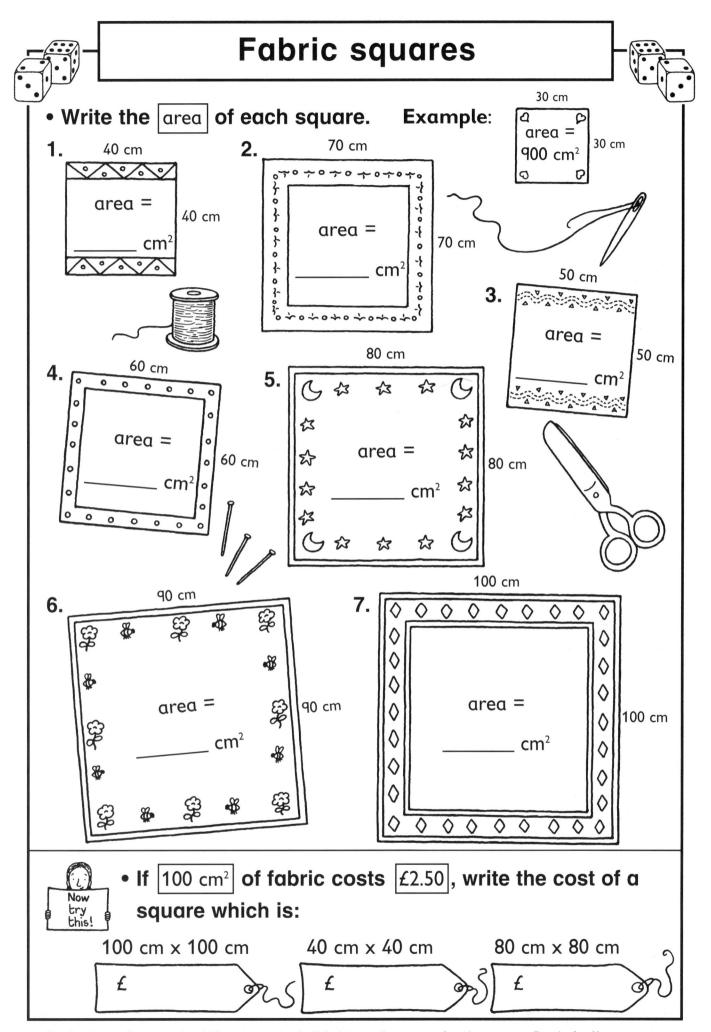

Teachers' note Encourage the children to recognise the links between the squares of numbers from 1 to 10, and the squares of the multiples of 10. Also point out that if the sides of a square are increased ten-fold, then the area increases one hundred-fold.

Developing Numeracy
Calculations Year 6
© A & C Black

35

Cut the ribbon

Each length of ribbon will be cut exactly in half.

• Write the length of each half.

1. 0·86 m — _0.43_ m
2. 1·14 m — _____ m
3. 0·78 m — _____ m
4. 1·88 m — _____ m
5. 0·58 m — _____ m
6. 1·52 m — _____ m
7. 1·72 m — _____ m
8. 1·34 m — _____ m
9. 1·44 m — _____ m

• Write the original length of the ribbon
  if a half is:

10. 0·92 m — _1.84_ m
11. 0·68 m — _____ m
12. 0·26 m — _____ m
13. 0·54 m — _____ m
14. 0·82 m — _____ m
15. 0·78 m — _____ m

These lengths of ribbon will be cut into quarters.

• Write the length of each quarter.

1·92 m _____ m   1·56 m _____ m

Teachers' note Help the children to appreciate that doubling and halving these numbers is similar to doubling and halving two- or three-digit numbers. When halving, they can halve the tenths first (including a units digit), then the hundredths.

**Developing Numeracy
Calculations Year 6
© A & C Black**

Double or nothing

• **Play this game with a partner.**

P.C. ✓

108	136	198	128	168	92
170	90	190	154	116	192
118	194	96	172	110	134
152	130	178	88	158	196
174	112	148	188	132	150
94	138	98	156	114	176

☆ Write the digits 4, 5, 6, 7, 8, 9 on each cube.
☆ Choose which colour cube will be the tens digit, and which the units digit.
☆ Take turns to roll the cubes to make a two-digit number. Double the number.
☆ If you can find the answer on the screen, cover it with a counter. Check each other's doubling.
☆ The winner is the first to get three in a line.

You need:
• two different-coloured cubes
• counters in two colours

Teachers' note The children can roll the tens digit first, for example 6, and say the double of 6 tens, i.e. one hundred and twenty. Then they roll the units digit, for example 7, and double this, i.e. fourteen, before adding them mentally to give the answer (134).

**Developing Numeracy
Calculations Year 6
© A & C Black**

Shoe shops

• **Write how many pairs of shoes are in each shop.**

1.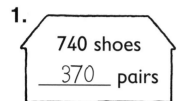
740 shoes
_370_ pairs

2.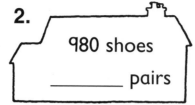
980 shoes
_____ pairs

3.
1460 shoes
_____ pairs

4.
1660 shoes
_____ pairs

5.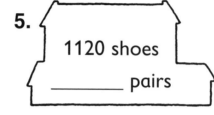
1120 shoes
_____ pairs

6.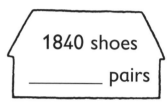
1840 shoes
_____ pairs

7.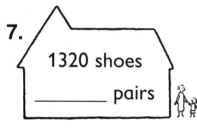
1320 shoes
_____ pairs

8.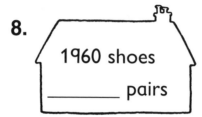
1960 shoes
_____ pairs

9.
1520 shoes
_____ pairs

• **Write how many shoes are being delivered.**

10.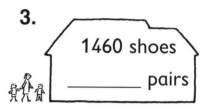
840 pairs
_____ shoes

11.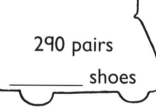
760 pairs
_____ shoes

12.
290 pairs
_____ shoes

13.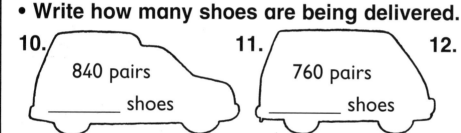
870 pairs
_____ shoes

14.
490 pairs
_____ shoes

15.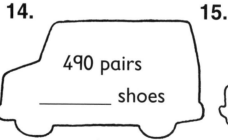
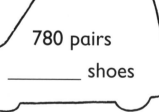
780 pairs
_____ shoes

Now try this!

Each pair of shoes is in a box. In each box there is also a spare pair of laces.

• **Write the total number of laces in:**

460 boxes	370 boxes	190 boxes	240 boxes
_____ laces	_____ laces	_____ laces	_____ laces
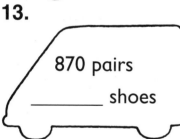

Teachers' note Help the children to appreciate that doubling and halving these numbers is similar to doubling and halving two- or three-digit numbers. To solve the extension activity, the children will need to double the numbers twice.

**Developing Numeracy
Calculations Year 6
© A & C Black**

Maths Mega-brain Quiz

The contestants must choose answer a , b or c .

A correct answer doubles their winnings.

An incorrect answer halves their winnings.

• Shade the correct letter. Write the final winnings.

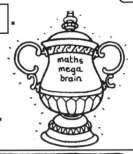

1. 4·3 x 10 is..?
a 0·43 [b] 43 c 430

winnings so far
£4 600

final winnings
£9 200

b

2. 2·78 x 100 is..?
a 278 b 27·8 c 2780

winnings so far
£8 400

final winnings

c

3. 5·61 x 10 is..?
a 56·1 b 561 c 0·561

winnings so far
£7 800

final winnings

c

4. 8·7 ÷ 10 is..?
a 870 b 0·87 c 87

winnings so far
£7 300

final winnings

c

5. 83·6 ÷ 100 is..?
a 83·6 b 836 c 0·836

winnings so far
£8 700

final winnings

c

6. 0·49 x 100 is..?
a 4·9 b 49 c 490

winnings so far
£158 000

final winnings

a

• **Write your winnings.**

You have £800 so far.

You answer the next six

questions correctly.

final winnings

You have £800 so far.

You answer the next five

questions incorrectly.

final winnings

Teachers' note To help the children answer the quiz questions, they may need reminding of the rules for multiplying and dividing by 10 and 100.

**Developing Numeracy
Calculations Year 6
© A & C Black**

Doubling and halving machine

This machine makes difficult multiplications easy.

15 × 18

If the units digit is **5**, put the number into the 'doubling' part of the machine.

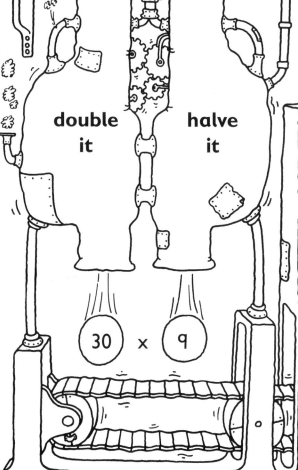

double it

halve it

30 × 9

- **Use the machine to help you complete these multiplications.**

1. 15 x 18 → __30__ x __9__ = __270__

2. 25 x 14 → ____ x ____ = ____

3. 35 x 16 → ____ x ____ = ____

4. 45 x 12 → ____ x ____ = ____

5. 25 x 18 → ____ x ____ = ____

6. 15 x 16 → ____ x ____ = ____

7. 55 x 12 → ____ x ____ = ____

8. 24 x 35 → ____ x ____ = ____

9. 18 x 45 → ____ x ____ = ____

Now try this!

- **Find the area of each rectangle.**
- **Write the calculation inside the rectangle.**

25 cm

16 cm

22 cm

15 cm

35 cm

18 cm

Teachers' note As a further extension, the method can be used to multiply numbers not ending in 5. Help the children to appreciate that the method is applicable only when at least one of the numbers is even. This number must be chosen to be halved. Demonstrate using factors why the method works, for example 25 x 14 = 25 x 2 x 7 = 50 x 7.

Developing Numeracy Calculations Year 6 © A & C Black

Cross-country race

Each school enters 15 **runners.**

- **Write how many runners are in the race if there are:**

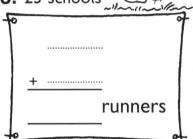

For 7 x 15,
find 7 x 10 ➝ 70
halve it ⟶ 35
and add ➝ 105

1. 18 schools

.....180. (18 x 10)

+ .....90. (halve it)

270 runners

2. 27 schools

....

+ ....

runners

3. 23 schools

....

+ ....

runners

4. 16 schools

....

+ ....

runners

5. 45 schools

....

+ ....

runners

6. 34 schools

....

+ ....

runners

- **Try a different method for these.**

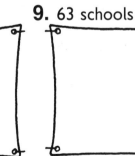

For 7 x 15,
find 7 x 30 ⟶ 210
then halve it ➝ 105

7. 17 schools

8. 24 schools

9. 63 schools

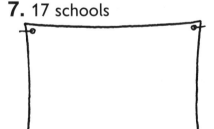

- **Find your own method for** x 35 .
- **Try it on these calculations.**

14 x 35   21 x 35

Teachers' note The children can use a calculator to check their answers to the calculations.
A solution to the extension activity is: step 1: x10, step 2: multiply this by 3, step 3: halve the x10,
step 4: add.

**Developing Numeracy
Calculations Year 6**
© A & C Black

Match tickets

A coach ticket costs $\boxed{£50}$ **.**

• **Write the total cost for:**

To multiply by 50,
multiply by 100,
then halve the answer.

1. 28 people

$$\frac{28 \times 100}{28 \times 50} = \underline{\hspace{2cm}}$$
$$= \underline{\hspace{2cm}}$$

2. 43 people

$$\underline{\hspace{3cm}} = \underline{\hspace{2cm}}$$
$$\underline{\hspace{3cm}} = \underline{\hspace{2cm}}$$

19 people
19 × 100 = 1900
19 × 50 = £950

3. 39 people

$$\underline{\hspace{3cm}} = \underline{\hspace{1.5cm}}$$
$$\underline{\hspace{3cm}} = \underline{\hspace{1.5cm}}$$

4. 112 people

$$\underline{\hspace{3cm}} = \underline{\hspace{1.5cm}}$$
$$\underline{\hspace{3cm}} = \underline{\hspace{1.5cm}}$$

5. 54 people

$$\underline{\hspace{3cm}} = \underline{\hspace{1.5cm}}$$
$$\underline{\hspace{3cm}} = \underline{\hspace{1.5cm}}$$

A match ticket costs $\boxed{£25}$ **.**

• **Write the total cost of:**

To multiply by 25,
multiply by 100,
halve the answer,
then halve it again.

6. 34 tickets

$$\frac{34 \times 100}{34 \times 50} = \underline{\hspace{1.5cm}}$$
$$\frac{34 \times 50}{34 \times 25} = \underline{\hspace{1.5cm}}$$
$$34 \times 25 = \underline{\hspace{1.5cm}}$$

7. 46 tickets

$$\underline{\hspace{3cm}} = \underline{\hspace{1.5cm}}$$
$$\underline{\hspace{3cm}} = \underline{\hspace{1.5cm}}$$
$$\underline{\hspace{3cm}} = \underline{\hspace{1.5cm}}$$

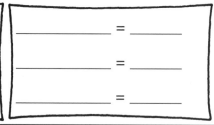

22 tickets
22 × 100 = 2200
22 × 50 = 1100
22 × 25 = £550

8. 17 tickets

$$\underline{\hspace{3cm}} = \underline{\hspace{1.5cm}}$$
$$\underline{\hspace{3cm}} = \underline{\hspace{1.5cm}}$$
$$\underline{\hspace{3cm}} = \underline{\hspace{1.5cm}}$$

9. 37 tickets

$$\underline{\hspace{3cm}} = \underline{\hspace{1.5cm}}$$
$$\underline{\hspace{3cm}} = \underline{\hspace{1.5cm}}$$
$$\underline{\hspace{3cm}} = \underline{\hspace{1.5cm}}$$

10. 59 tickets

$$\underline{\hspace{3cm}} = \underline{\hspace{1.5cm}}$$
$$\underline{\hspace{3cm}} = \underline{\hspace{1.5cm}}$$
$$\underline{\hspace{3cm}} = \underline{\hspace{1.5cm}}$$

Now
try
this!

Match tickets are $\boxed{\text{half price}}$ **for children.**

• **Write the total cost of tickets for:**

$\boxed{\text{28 children}}$ \underline{\hspace{1.5cm}} $\boxed{\text{46 children}}$ \underline{\hspace{1.5cm}} $\boxed{\text{84 children}}$ \underline{\hspace{1.5cm}}

Teachers' note Explain to the children that a method of dividing by 4 is to halve, then halve again. This strategy can be extended to dividing by 8.

**Developing Numeracy
Calculations Year 6
© A & C Black**

Multiplication tables

- **Fill in the** $\boxed{\times 6}$ **table. Then complete the others by doubling.**

1 x 6 = _____	1 x 12 = _____	1 x 24 = _____
2 x 6 = _____	2 x 12 = _____	2 x 24 = _____
3 x 6 = _____	3 x 12 = _____	3 x 24 = _____
4 x 6 = _____	4 x 12 = _____	4 x 24 = _____
5 x 6 = _____	5 x 12 = _____	5 x 24 = _____
6 x 6 = _____	6 x 12 = _____	6 x 24 = _____
7 x 6 = _____	7 x 12 = _____	7 x 24 = _____
8 x 6 = _____	8 x 12 = _____	8 x 24 = _____
9 x 6 = _____	9 x 12 = _____	9 x 24 = _____
10 x 6 = _____	10 x 12 = _____	10 x 24 = _____

- **Fill in the** $\boxed{\times 7}$ **table.**

1 x 7 = _____
2 x 7 = _____
3 x 7 = _____
4 x 7 = _____
5 x 7 = _____
6 x 7 = _____
7 x 7 = _____
8 x 7 = _____
9 x 7 = _____
10 x 7 = _____

- **Use the** $\boxed{\times 7}$ **table to find how many items are in the boxes.**

1.
14 candles

9 boxes

_____ candles

2.
28 candles

6 boxes

_____ candles

3.
14 bulbs

5 boxes

_____ bulbs

4.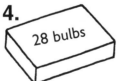
28 bulbs

7 boxes

_____ bulbs

5.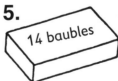
14 baubles

6 boxes

_____ baubles

6.
28 baubles

8 boxes

_____ baubles

Now try this!

- **Use** $\boxed{3 \times 8 = 24}$ **and** $\boxed{6 \times 9 = 54}$ **to help you find these answers.**

3 x 16 = _____   6 x 18 = _____

3 x 32 = _____   6 x 36 = _____

Teachers' note This doubling strategy should give children confidence that once they know their multiplication tables up to 10, they can derive much harder multiplications from them.

Developing Numeracy Calculations Year 6 © A & C Black

Night out

- **Complete the tables by doubling.**
- **Use a calculator to check your results.**

1 x 26 = _26_	1 x 31 = _____	1 x 37 = _____
2 x 26 = _52_	2 x 31 = _____	2 x 37 = _____
4 x 26 = _____	4 x 31 = _____	4 x 37 = _____
8 x 26 = _____	8 x 31 = _____	8 x 37 = _____
16 x 26 = _____	16 x 31 = _____	16 x 37 = _____

- **Use the tables above to find the cost of the tickets.**

Pop concert £37 per ticket

Three of us !!!
Sold out!

	cost
	cost
12 tickets	£
24 tickets	£
11 tickets	£

Musical £26 per ticket

CAT

	cost
	cost
9 tickets	£
17 tickets	£
14 tickets	£

Panto £31 per ticket

Jack & the Beanstalk

	cost
	cost
5 tickets	£
7 tickets	£
28 tickets	£

Now try this!

- **Use the tables above to help you find these answers.**

26 x 26 = _____   31 x 31 = _____

Teachers' note Challenge the children to use the tables to find harder linked multiplications, for example 115 x 37, 129 x 26. Demonstrate how to use a combination of table facts, for example to find 12 x 26, they can combine 4 x 26 and 8 x 26. The children can check the tables using a calculator before moving on to finding the cost of the tickets.

Developing Numeracy Calculations Year 6 © A & C Black

Martian multiplication

1	2	3	4	5	6	7	8	9	10
2	4	6	8	10	12	14	16	18	20
3	6	9	12	15	18	21	24	27	30
4	8	12	16	20	24	28	32	36	40
5	10	15	20	25	30	35	40	45	50
6	12	18	24	30	36	42	48	54	60
7	14	21	28	35	(42)	49	56	63	70
8	16	24	32	40	48	56	64	72	80
9	18	27	36	45	54	63	72	81	90
10	20	30	40	50	(60)	70	80	90	100

To find 6 x 17, look for 6 x 7 and 6 x 10, then add.

• **Use the table to complete these multiplications.**

1. 6 x 17 = $\underline{42 + 60 = 102}$

2. 4 x 16 = _____

3. 7 x 18 = _____

4. 3 x 19 = _____

5. 8 x 12 = _____

6. 5 x 13 = _____

7. 9 x 14 = _____

8. 7 x 17 = _____

9. 8 x 19 = _____

10. 8 x 16 = _____

11. 9 x 18 = _____

12. 7 x 19 = _____

Now try this!

• **Use the** $\boxed{\times 12}$ **ladder to help you complete these.**

13 x 12 = _____

17 x 12 = _____

11 x 12 = _____

19 x 12 = _____

12
24
36
48
60
72
84
96
108
120

Teachers' note The children can be encouraged to extend the use of the multiplication square, for example multiplying 7 x 27 by doubling 7 x 10 and adding 7 x 7.

**Developing Numeracy
Calculations Year 6
© A & C Black**

101 Dalmatians

- **Write the number of spots on 101 Dalmatians, if each dog has:**

Multiply by 100, then add one dog's spots.

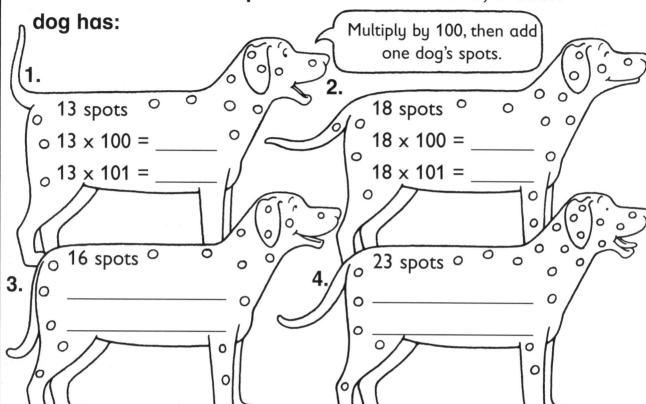

1.
13 spots
13 x 100 = _____
13 x 101 = _____

2.
18 spots
18 x 100 = _____
18 x 101 = _____

3.
16 spots
_____
_____

4.
23 spots
_____
_____

Two of the dogs are off their food.

- **How many dog treats a week do you need for 99 dogs, if each dog has:**

5.
14 treats a week
14 x 100 = _____
14 x 99 = _____

Multiply by 100, then subtract one dog's treats.

6.
12 treats a week
_____
_____

7.
21 treats a week
_____
_____

8.
19 treats a week
_____
_____

Now try this!

- **If each Dalmatian has 14 spots, how many spots are there on:** 201 dogs? _____   199 dogs? _____

Teachers' note Encourage the children to derive similar strategies for other multiplications, for example x201, x198.

**Developing Numeracy
Calculations Year 6
© A & C Black**

Packets of paperclips

'Clipwell' sell paperclips in boxes of 51.

- Write how many paperclips each teacher has.

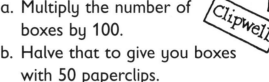

a. Multiply the number of boxes by 100.
b. Halve that to give you boxes with 50 paperclips.
c. Add one more paperclip per box.

1.

46 boxes

a. 46 × 100 = 4600
b. 46 × 50 = 2300
c. 46 × 51 = 2346

2.

18 boxes

3.

35 boxes

4.

27 boxes

'Griptight' sell paperclips in boxes of 49.

- Write how many paperclips each teacher has.

Instead of adding a paperclip for each box, this time subtract one for each box.

5.

28 boxes

6.

16 boxes

7.

39 boxes

8.

42 boxes

- Write how many more 'Clipwell' paperclips you have than 'Griptight' ones if you buy:

| 29 boxes of each | 53 boxes of each |

Teachers' note Before beginning the activity, remind the children of strategies for multiplying by 50, for example multiplying by 100, then halving. The space for working out has been left blank to allow for flexibility in the methods the children use for calculating.

**Developing Numeracy
Calculations Year 6
© A & C Black**

a, b or c?

- **Estimate the answer and write** a , b **or** c .
- **Multiply to find the answer.**
  Write the correct letter.

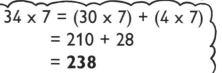
$$34 \times 7 = (30 \times 7) + (4 \times 7)$$
$$= 210 + 28$$
$$= \textbf{238}$$

1.

46 × 7	
a	292
b	322
c	342

estimate	answer

workings

2.

38 × 8	
a	326
b	244
c	304

estimate	answer

workings

3.

57 × 9	
a	513
b	423
c	583

estimate	answer

workings

4.

89 × 4	
a	356
b	436
c	276

estimate	answer

workings

5.

68 × 6	
a	528
b	328
c	408

estimate	answer

workings

6.

74 × 8	
a	584
b	592
c	606

estimate	answer

workings

Now try this!

- **Estimate the order of the answers, smallest to largest.**

  x 86 × 7   y 76 × 8   z 87 × 6

- **Multiply them to check**
  the actual order.

estimated order			
actual order			

Teachers' note When estimating, some children may feel confident enough to calculate the accurate answer very quickly. Others will need to round the two-digit number to its nearest multiple of 10. The children could do the activity in pairs, comparing their estimates and answers, and checking with a calculator if their answers do not match.

Developing Numeracy
Calculations Year 6
© A & C Black

Formula One digits

- **Use the digits** $\boxed{1}$, $\boxed{2}$, $\boxed{4}$, $\boxed{7}$ **and** $\boxed{8}$
to make these decimal multiplications.

> Look at the last digit of the answer.

1.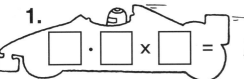
$\boxed{} \cdot \boxed{} \times \boxed{} =$ **4·8**

2.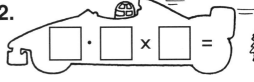
$\boxed{} \cdot \boxed{} \times \boxed{} =$ **9·4**

3.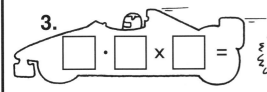
$\boxed{} \cdot \boxed{} \times \boxed{} =$ **56·8**

4.
$\boxed{} \cdot \boxed{} \times \boxed{} =$ **32·8**

5.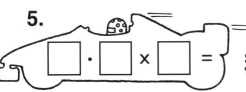
$\boxed{} \cdot \boxed{} \times \boxed{} =$ **19·6**

6.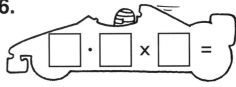
$\boxed{} \cdot \boxed{} \times \boxed{} =$ **59·2**

- **Complete these using the digits** $\boxed{1}$, $\boxed{3}$, $\boxed{5}$, $\boxed{6}$ **and** $\boxed{9}$.

7.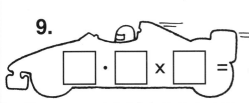
$\boxed{} \cdot \boxed{} \times \boxed{} =$ **15·3**

8.
$\boxed{} \cdot \boxed{} \times \boxed{} =$ **31·5**

9.
$\boxed{} \cdot \boxed{} \times \boxed{} =$ **54·6**

10.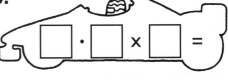
$\boxed{} \cdot \boxed{} \times \boxed{} =$ **58·5**

11.
$\boxed{} \cdot \boxed{} \times \boxed{} =$ **47·7**

12.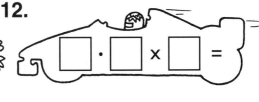
$\boxed{} \cdot \boxed{} \times \boxed{} =$ **11·4**

Now try this!

- **Use the digits** $\boxed{2}$, $\boxed{3}$, $\boxed{4}$, $\boxed{6}$ **and** $\boxed{8}$ **to make 14·4. Find three different ways.**

$\boxed{} \cdot \boxed{} \times \boxed{} = 14\cdot4$

$\boxed{} \cdot \boxed{} \times \boxed{} = 14\cdot4$

$\boxed{} \cdot \boxed{} \times \boxed{} = 14\cdot4$

Teachers' note Discuss strategies for completing the calculations with the children. One strategy is to look at the size of the product, then to look for appropriate digits for the multiplier. Another clue is given in the units digit of the product.

**Developing Numeracy
Calculations Year 6
© A & C Black**

Four facts

The product of 0·65 and 4 is 2·6.

When 9·94 is divided by 7, the answer is 1·42.

9·6 is 12 times 0·8.

An eighth of 2·8 is 0·35.

• **Use the four facts above to complete these calculations.**

1. 2·6 ÷ 4 = _____

2. 1·42 x 7 = _____

3. 9·6 ÷ 12 = _____

4. 4 x 0·65 = _____

5. 0·8 x 12 = _____

6. 9·6 ÷ 0·8 = _____

7. 7 x 1·42 = _____

8. 9·94 ÷ 1·42 = _____

9. 2·6 ÷ 0·65 = _____

10. 2·8 ÷ 0·35 = _____

11. 0·35 x 8 = _____

12. one-quarter of 2·6 = _____

13. one-seventh of 9·94 = _____

14. one-twelfth of 9·6 = _____

• **Find two division and two multiplication facts from this statement. Write them in words.** $\frac{1}{5}$ of 16 = 3·2

When 16 is divided by _____

_____

_____

_____

Teachers' note The children may need support when creating multiplication statements from statements like 'an eighth of 2·8 is 0·35'. They need to relate this to 2·8 ÷ 8. The children could time themselves when answering the questions.

**Developing Numeracy
Calculations Year 6
© A & C Black**

Number Cruncher

The Number Cruncher is eating the multiplications.

- Fill in the missing numbers.

1. 2·43 x 100 = 243

2. 5·63 x 10 =

3. 7·6 x 100 =

4. 8·4 x 100 =

5. 2·5 x 10 =

6. 3·76 x 100 =

7. 4·8 x ⬚ = 48

8. 2·64 x ⬚ = 26·4

9. 7·35 x ⬚ = 735

10. 5·8 x ⬚ = 580

11. 0·9 x ⬚ = 9

12. 3·06 x ⬚ = 30·6

13. ⬚ x 100 = 409

14. ⬚ x 10 = 27·8

Now try this!

The Number Cruncher buys some new clothes.

- Write the cost of 10 of each item.

£3.25   £4.78   £5.75   £6.49

For money, you need two decimal places. (£32.50 not £32.5)

cost of 10: £ _____   £ _____   £ _____   £ _____

Teachers' note The children can check the multiplications by using number cards on a place-value board, sliding them to the left to multiply by 10 or 100. The children will need to discuss where it is necessary to use zero as a placeholder, for example 8·4 x 100 = 840.

**Developing Numeracy
Calculations Year 6
© A & C Black**

Divine divisions

Cruncher Divine is devouring the divisions.

- **Fill in the missing numbers.**

1. $64 \div 100 =$ 0.64

2. $73 \div 100 =$ ___

3. $7 \div 100 =$ ___

4. $9 \div 100 =$ ___

5. $28 \div 10 =$ ___

6. $64 \div 10 =$ ___

7. $4 \div$ ___ $= 0.4$

8. $3 \div$ ___ $= 0.03$

9. $68 \div$ ___ $= 0.68$

10. $72 \div$ ___ $= 7.2$

11. ___ $\div 10 = 0.1$

12. ___ $\div 100 = 0.06$

13. ___ $\div 10 = 1.7$

14. ___ $\div 100 = 0.93$

 **• Write the length in metres of each Cruncher sock.**

     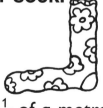

3 cm   170 mm   24 cm $\frac{1}{4}$ of a metre

_____ m   _____ m   _____ m   _____ m

Teachers' note The children can check the divisions by using number cards on a place-value board, sliding them to the right to divide by 10 or 100. The children need to be confident in using zero as a placeholder. Encourage them to put zero in the units column, i.e. to write 0·64 rather than ·64.

**Developing Numeracy
Calculations Year 6
© A & C Black**

Parachute game

• **Play this game with a partner. Take it in turns.**

☆ Shuffle the number cards. Spread them face down.

☆ Choose a decimal number from the landing pads. Then turn over a number card. Multiply them together.

☆ If the answer is on a parachute, cover it with a counter.

☆ Check each other's answers. Use a calculator if necessary.

☆ Replace the number card face down.

☆ The winner is the player who covers the most parachutes.

You need:
• number cards 1 to 9
• 30 counters in two colours
• a calculator

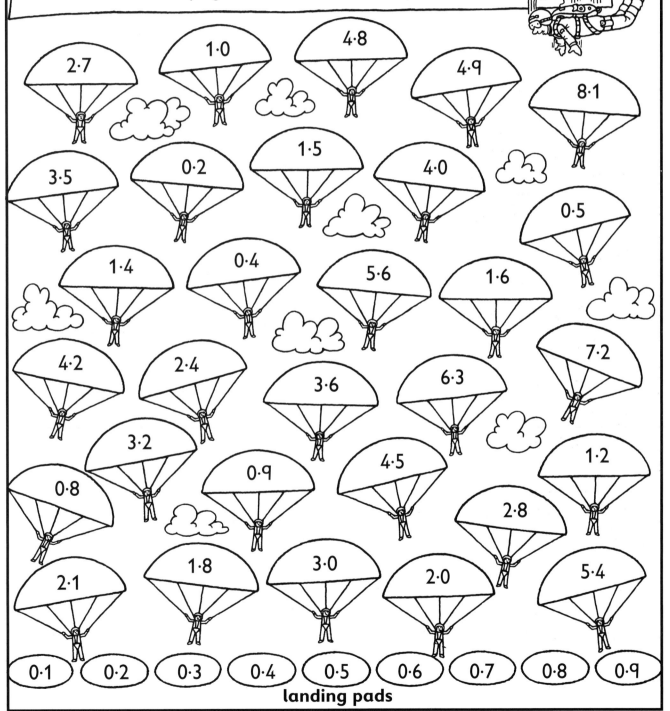

2·7   1·0   4·8   4·9   8·1

3·5   0·2   1·5   4·0   0·5

1·4   0·4   5·6   1·6

4·2   2·4   3·6   6·3   7·2

3·2   0·9   4·5   1·2   2·8

0·8   2·1   1·8   3·0   2·0   5·4

landing pads

| 0·1 | 0·2 | 0·3 | 0·4 | 0·5 | 0·6 | 0·7 | 0·8 | 0·9 |

Teachers' note Invite the children to investigate any possible products which do not appear on a parachute.

Developing Numeracy Calculations Year 6 © A & C Black

53

Grid multiplication

- **Use the grids to help you complete the multiplications.**
- **Make an estimate first.**

1. 5642 x 3

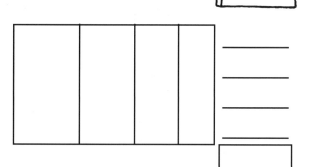

estimate
16000

	5000	600	40	2
3	15000	1800	120	6

15000
1800
120
6

2. 1938 x 4

estimate

---

3. 6385 x 5

estimate

---

4. 3296 x 3

estimate

---

5. 4756 x 4

estimate

---

6. 3726 x 7

estimate

- **Find the multiplication shown by this grid.**

28000	4900	140	56

28000
4900
140
56

_____ x _____ = _____

Teachers' note Practise rounding a four-digit number to its nearest thousand so that children can use this to estimate the products, for example 4756 x 4 is approximately 5000 x 4 = 20000. Since 4756 is less than 5000 by about 250, a better estimate is one which takes this into account, for example 19000 (20000 less 4 x 250).

**Developing Numeracy
Calculations Year 6
© A & C Black**

More grid multiplication

- **Use the grid method to complete these multiplications.**
- **Make an estimate first.**

1. 356 × 23

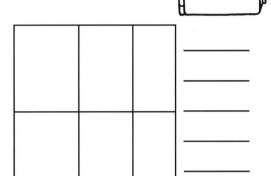

estimate
7000

	300	50	6
20	6000	1000	120
3	900	150	18

6000
1000
120
900
150
18

2. 427 × 31

estimate

---

3. 548 × 17

 estimate

4. 635 × 27

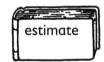 estimate

---

Now try this!

- **Use the digits** 1 , 2 , 3 , 4 **and** 5 **to make a three-digit number and a two-digit number.**
- **Which choice will give the largest answer when they are multiplied together?**

You must use all five digits.

Use the grid method.

_____ x _____ = _____

Teachers' note In the extension activity, the children need to try different options on paper. Discuss strategies for this, for example putting the largest digits in the hundreds and tens places.

**Developing Numeracy
Calculations Year 6
© A & C Black**

Brains versus calculators!

• Follow the instructions.

☆ Start the timer. Check the ten multiplications using a pencil and paper. Show your workings.

☆ Mark each multiplication with a $\boxed{✓}$ or a $\boxed{✗}$. Write down your time.

☆ Now check them again using a calculator. Time how long it takes this time.

You need:
- a timer
- pencil and paper
- a calculator

1. 4346 x 7 = 30422   ☐ ✏ ☐ 🖩

2. 5136 x 4 = 20544   ☐ ✏ ☐ 🖩

3. 2749 x 5 = 13845   ☐ ✏ ☐ 🖩

4. 3874 x 6 = 13232   ☐ ✏ ☐ 🖩

5. 5134 x 8 = 41072   ☐ ✏ ☐ 🖩

6. 4158 x 3 = 12454   ☐ ✏ ☐ 🖩

7. 2736 x 9 = 26624   ☐ ✏ ☐ 🖩

8. 7152 x 6 = 42912   ☐ ✏ ☐ 🖩

9. 3827 x 4 = 15208   ☐ ✏ ☐ 🖩

10. 3194 x 7 = 22358   ☐ ✏ ☐ 🖩

∕ 10

• Which did you find:

easiest? ☐ ✏ ☐ 🖩

fastest? ☐ ✏ ☐ 🖩

most accurate? ☐ ✏ ☐ 🖩

• Choose three of the multiplications with wrong answers. Write them correctly.

Teachers' note In order to find the mistakes, the children will need to work carefully through each calculation. They should record their workings on a separate sheet of paper. Discuss the advantages and disadvantages of using calculators.

Developing Numeracy Calculations Year 6
© A & C Black

Long multiplication

Each multiplication uses the digits $\boxed{2}$, $\boxed{3}$, $\boxed{4}$, $\boxed{5}$ and $\boxed{6}$.

• Estimate the multiplication, then complete it.

1. estimate _12000_

```
    5 6 4
  x   2 3
  ─────────
  1 1 2 8 0   (564 x 20)
    1 6 9 2   (564 x 3)
  ─────────
  1 2 9 7 2
        1
```

2. estimate _____

```
    4 3 5
  x   2 6
  ─────────
          (        )
          (        )
  ─────────
```

3. estimate _____

```
    2 6 4
  x   5 3
  ─────────
          (        )
          (        )
  ─────────
```

4. estimate _____

```
    5 3 2
  x   4 6
  ─────────
          (        )
          (        )
  ─────────
```

5. estimate _____

```
    2 3 6
  x   4 5
  ─────────
          (        )
          (        )
  ─────────
```

6. estimate _____

```
    4 5 6
  x   3 2
  ─────────
          (        )
          (        )
  ─────────
```

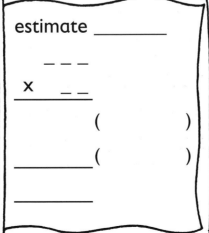

• Use the digits above to make multiplications with answers close to $\boxed{10\,000}$, $\boxed{20\,000}$ and $\boxed{30\,000}$.

estimate _____

```
    _ _ _
  x   _ _
  ─────────
          (        )
          (        )
  ─────────
```

estimate _____

```
    _ _ _
  x   _ _
  ─────────
          (        )
          (        )
  ─────────
```

estimate _____

```
    _ _ _
  x   _ _
  ─────────
          (        )
          (        )
  ─────────
```

Teachers' note Revise methods for multiplying by 20, for example multiplying by 10, then by 2 (which can be done by writing a zero in the units place, before multiplying by 2). In the extension activity, encourage the children to think about the hundreds digit of the three-digit number and the tens digit of the two-digit number (for example, for an answer close to 10 000 try 4_ _ x 2 _, as 400 x 20 = 8000).

**Developing Numeracy
Calculations Year 6
© A & C Black**

Estimating and multiplying

- Estimate the answers to the multiplications.
- Put your estimates in order, smallest to largest, using the letters.

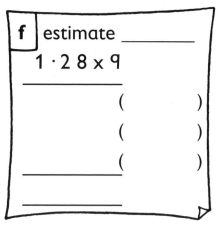

estimated order						
actual order						

- Complete the multiplications.

a estimate ___14·7___

4 · 92 x 3

12 · 00	(4·00 x 3)
2 · 70	(0·90 x 3)
0 · 06	(0·02 x 3)
14 · 76	

b estimate _____

3 · 16 x 7

	(3·00 x 7)
	(0·10 x 7)
	(0·06 x 7)

c estimate _____

3 · 27 x 5

	(3·00 x 5)
	(0·20 x 5)
	(0·07 x 5)

d estimate _____

4 · 93 x 4

	(x 4)
	(x 4)
	(x 4)

e estimate _____

2 · 58 x 6

	( )
	( )
	( )

f estimate _____

1 · 28 x 9

	( )
	( )
	( )

- Write the actual order. Compare it with your estimate.

Now try this!

- Estimate the difference between the answers to these multiplications. 2·88 x 5 | 3·24 x 6
- Work them out. Then subtract one answer from the other to find the actual difference.

estimated difference _____   actual difference _____

Teachers' note The estimates of the size of the six multiplications can be made by rounding each decimal number to the nearest whole number, then multiplying and adjusting slightly, for example 4·92 x 3 is a little less than 5 x 3, say approximately 14·7.

Developing Numeracy Calculations Year 6 © A & C Black

Sports Day

The schools are dividing children into teams.

- **Calculate the number of teams.**
- **First, write an estimate in the star.**

1.  Longbarrow Primary

768 pupils
32 per team ☆ 25

```
      24 teams
32 | 7 6 8
   -  6 4 0  (20 × 32)
      1 2 8
   -  1 2 8  (4 × 32)
          0
```

2.  The Lion School

621 pupils
23 per team ☆

☐ teams

3.  St Mary's Primary

594 pupils
18 per team ☆

☐ teams

4. Rosewood School

943 pupils
41 per team ☆

☐ teams

5. Greatkids Primary

806 pupils
31 per team ☆

☐ teams

6. The Lark School

1092 pupils
26 per team ☆

☐ teams

- **For questions 1, 2 and 3, divide the number of pupils by the number of teams.**

  Example: 1. 24 | 768

- **What do you notice?** _____

  _____

Teachers' note The children should be encouraged to check their calculations using an inverse, i.e. a multiplication: 32 × 24 in question 1. The extension activity consolidates the concept of two linking division facts, for example 768 ÷ 32 = 24 and 768 ÷ 24 = 32.

**Developing Numeracy
Calculations Year 6
© A & C Black**

Checking divisions

• **Check each division by doing the** $\boxed{\text{inverse}}$ **(multiplying).**

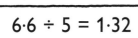

Inverse means **opposite**.

$6 \cdot 6 \div 5 = 1 \cdot 32$ check $1 \cdot 32 \times 5 =$ _____ workings	$19 \div 4 = 4 \cdot 75$ check $4 \cdot 75 \times 4 =$ _____ workings	$32 \cdot 3 \div 5 = 6 \cdot 46$ check $6 \cdot 46 \times 5 =$ _____ workings
$44 \cdot 1 \div 6 = 7 \cdot 35$ check _____ $\times 6 =$ _____ workings	$\frac{1}{4}$ of $24 \cdot 6 = 6 \cdot 15$ check _____ $\times 4 =$ _____ workings	$\frac{1}{8}$ of $30 \cdot 8 = 3 \cdot 85$ check _____ $\times 8 =$ _____ workings

• **Check these halves by doing the inverse (doubling).**

$\frac{1}{2}$ of $7 \cdot 1 = 3 \cdot 55$ check double $3 \cdot 55 =$ _____ workings	$\frac{1}{2}$ of $5 \cdot 3 = 2 \cdot 65$ check double _____ $=$ _____ workings	$\frac{1}{2}$ of $3 \cdot 7 = 1 \cdot 85$ check double _____ $=$ _____ workings

---

Now try this!

• **Check these calculations by multiplying by 4 (doubling, then doubling again).**

$\frac{1}{4}$ of $10 \cdot 8 = 2 \cdot 7$	$\frac{1}{4}$ of $4 \cdot 92 = 1 \cdot 23$	$\frac{1}{4}$ of $22 \cdot 96 = 5 \cdot 74$

Teachers' note Help the children to gain experience in using an inverse as a check by frequently asking them to use this method.

**Developing Numeracy
Calculations Year 6**
© A & C Black

Odd-Bod or Even-Steven?

• **Play this game with a partner.**

O stands for **odd**.

E stands for **even**.

☆ Decide who will be 'odd' and who 'even'.
☆ Cut out the cards. Spread them face down.

Game 1
☆ Take turns to reveal a card. If it is yours (for example, if you are 'odd' and the answer is odd), keep the card. If not, give it to your partner. Check each other's answers.

Game 2
☆ Take turns to reveal two cards. Add them together. Say 'odd' or 'even' for the total.

O x O	E x E	O x E
E x O	73 x 25	46 x 24
28 x 19	75 x 24	26 x 35 x 27
43 x 28 x 14	17 x 25 x 33	O – E
E – E	E – O	O – O
2719 – 832	4132 – 648	2748 – 539
1679 – 355	O + O + E	E + O + O
O + E + E	E + E + O	475 + 319 + 284
258 + 97 + 1493	2873 + 84 + 196	148 + 76 + 273

Teachers' note Follow up the activity by inviting the children to find how many of the cards have an odd answer and how many an even answer. They can check the answers using a calculator. The 'general' cards can be checked by investigating, in pairs, different chosen examples. Encourage the children to give a reason for any general observation, for example E x O = E.

**Developing Numeracy
Calculations Year 6
© A & C Black**

Answers

p6
1. 5, 6, 7
2. 11, 12, 13
3. 24, 25, 26
4. 3, 4, 5, 6
5. 9, 10, 11, 12
6. 7, 8, 9, 10
7. 2, 3, 4, 5, 6
8. 5, 6, 7, 8, 9
9. 18, 19, 20, 21, 22

p7
1. 71
2. 55
3. 79
4. 38
5. 74
6. 43
7. 73
8. 54
9. 75
10. 79
11. 37
12. 45

Now try this!
1871   1895   1591

p8
1. 401
2. 609
3. 208
4. 408
5. 511
6. 406
7. 204 boys, 196 girls
8. 288 boys, 312 girls
9. 110 boys, 100 girls
10. 246 boys, 262 girls

p9
1. 9·4 m
2. 15·5 m
3. 18·2 m
4. 12·4 m
5. 10·4 m
6. 20·5 m
7. 6·7 m
8. 8·8 m
9. 10·5 m
10. 11·5 m
11. 6·9 m
12. 8·6 m

Now try this!
8·7 m

p10
4·4 million   10·5 million   6·6 million
15·4 million   3·7 million   6·8 million
10·4 million   7·5 million   13·2 million

Now try this!
Home and Alone, by £6000

p11
Answers in lamp: 3·83   5·47
                   3·32   1·93

1. 2·73
2. 5·3
3. 0·8
4. 4·62
5. 2·47
6. 0·17
7. 1·3
8. 1·36
9. 4·73
10. 2·17
11. 1·47
12. 7·62

Now try this!
1·72 + 4·21 = 5·93   5·93 − 4·21 = 1·72   5·93 − 1·72 = 4·21
4·21 + 2·49 = 6·7   6·7 − 2·49 = 4·21   6·7 − 4·21 = 2·49
1·72 + 2·49 = 4·21   4·21 − 2·49 = 1·72   4·21 − 1·72 = 2·49

p12
Answers may vary.

(caterpillar diagrams: 120, 10, 30, 80 / 150, 20, 90, 40 / 220, 90, 50, 80, 140, 50, 70, 20 / 100, 20, 10, 40 / 160, 30, 10, 40, 80, 240, 50, 40, 90 / 210, 70, 30, 20, 40, 50, 240, 20, 90, 40, 60, 30, 60, 90)

Now try this!

(diagrams: 200, 20, 90, 90 / 200, 80, 90, 30 / 200, 60, 50, 70, 20 / 300, 50, 90, 70, 90, 60, 300, 60, 90, 20, 70)

p13
1. £79
2. £114
3. £105
4. £77
5. £94
6. £78
7. £87
8. £128
9. £149
10. £160
11. £140
12. £110

Now try this!
total 190

p14
1. 98 kg
2. 209 kg
3. 246 kg
4. 254 kg
Totals for rows are: 18, 61, 75, 134, 134, 265, 194, 294, 427, 473

Now try this!
Possibilities include:
51 + 52 + 55 = 158
30 + 31 + 32 + 34 = 127
51 + 52 + 53 + 54 + 55 = 265
71 + 72 + 73 + 74 + 75 + 79 = 444

p15

Name of attraction	Local visitors	Foreign visitors	Total
Tower of London	2300	5600	**7900**
Madam Tussauds	2700	6400	**9100**
Houses of Parliament	1900	6500	**8400**
Trafalgar Square	1700	7300	**9000**
London Zoo	2800	3900	**6700**
London Aquarium	4700	7400	**12100**
London Planetarium	2600	**4700**	7300
Buckingham Palace	3800	**5900**	9700
Natural History Museum	4900	**3700**	8600
10 Downing Street	1800	**4600**	6400
The London Eye	2300	**4900**	7200
St Paul's Cathedral	3200	**2900**	6100

Now try this!
2700, 5400   3100, 6200   4200, 8400

p17
1. 0·55 m
2. 0·28 m
3. 0·19 m
4. 0·64 m
5. 0·33 m
6. 0·71 m
7. 4·68 m
8. 8·28 m
9. 3·92 m

Now try this!
0·13 m

p18
2·43 + 0·07 = 2.5   2·43 + 0·57 = 3
2·78 + 0·02 = 2.8   2·78 + 0·22 = 3

5·38 + 0·02 = 5.4   5·38 + 0·62 = 6
5·81 + 0·09 = 5.9   5·81 + 0·19 = 6

1. 0·37
2. 0·73
3. 0·03
4. 0·04
5. 0·53
6. 0·92
7. 0·06
8. 0·07

p19

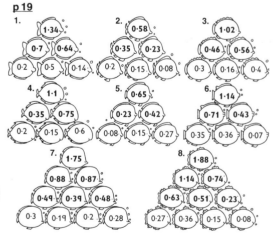

1. 1·34 / 0·7, 0·64 / 0·2, 0·5, 0·14
2. 0·58 / 0·35, 0·23 / 0·2, 0·15, 0·08
3. 1·02 / 0·46, 0·56 / 0·3, 0·16, 0·4
4. 1·1 / 0·35, 0·75 / 0·2, 0·15, 0·6
5. 0·65 / 0·23, 0·42 / 0·08, 0·15, 0·27
6. 1·14 / 0·71, 0·43 / 0·35, 0·36, 0·07
7. 1·75 / 0·88, 0·87 / 0·49, 0·39, 0·48 / 0·3, 0·19, 0·2, 0·28
8. 1·88 / 1·14, 0·74 / 0·63, 0·51, 0·23 / 0·27, 0·36, 0·15, 0·08

p20
1. 6534
2. 3604
3. 4120
4. 4612
5. 5715

Now try this!
Saturday 10138   Sunday 14447

Answers

p 21

Note that these answers may vary greatly, e.g. 6875 + 3421 gives the same answer as 8532 + 1764.

1. 3584 + 2617   **2.** 8532 + 1764   **3.** 8735 + 2164
4. 4637 + 5128   **5.** 1362 + 8547   **6.** 5368 + 2714
7. 4718 + 2356   **8.** 5318 + 2746   **9.** 3452 + 1678

Now try this!
Possible solutions: 8642 + 7531 = 16173
1357 + 2468 = 3825

p 22

1. £8800   **2.** £511   **3.** £799   **4.** £9591   **5.** £1302
6. £7599   **7.** £9311   **8.** £2519   **9.** £8062

p 24

1. 2869   **2.** 3658   **3.** 1336
4. 5675   **5.** 4302   **6.** 1189

Now try this!
5356 − 2869 = 2487   5832 − 3658 = 2174
4615 − 1336 = 3279
The answers match the number subtracted.

p 27

Answers will vary.

1. target 30 → (4 × 5) + 3 + 7

Now try this!

p 28

1. $18\frac{1}{2}$, $12\frac{1}{3}$, $9\frac{1}{4}$, $7\frac{2}{5}$, $6\frac{1}{6}$, $5\frac{2}{7}$, $4\frac{5}{8}$, $4\frac{1}{4}$, $3\frac{7}{10}$
2. 24, 16, 12, $9\frac{1}{3}$, 8, $6\frac{6}{7}$, 6, $5\frac{1}{3}$, $4\frac{4}{5}$
3. 40, $26\frac{2}{3}$, 20, 16, $13\frac{1}{3}$, $11\frac{3}{7}$, 10, $8\frac{8}{9}$, 8
4. 14, $9\frac{1}{3}$, 7, $5\frac{3}{5}$, $4\frac{2}{3}$, 4, $3\frac{1}{2}$, $3\frac{1}{9}$, $2\frac{4}{5}$

p 30

1. 6·12   6·0   6·2   6·5   6·25   b, a, c, e, d
2. 4·76   4·9   5·2   5·5   4·75   e, a, b, c, d
3. 2·12   2·1   2·6   2·5   2·25   b, a, e, d, c
4. 6·98   7·0   6·8   7·5   6·75   e, c, a, b, d
5. 9·10   8·9   9·2   8·5   8·75   d, e, b, a, c
6. 3·92   3·9   3·8   4·0   3·75   e, c, b, a, d

p 31

1. 6 × 7   **2.** 7 × 9
3. 3 × 9   **4.** 6 × 9
5. 2 × 4   **6.** 8 × 10

1, **2**, **3**, 4, **5**, **6**, **7**, 8, **9**, **10**, **12**, **14**, **15**, **16**, **18**, **20**, 21, **24**, **25**, 27, **28**, 30, **32**, **35**, **36**, **40**, 42, **45**, **48**, **49**, **50**, 54, **56**, **60**, 63, **64**, **70**, **72**, 80, **81**, **90**, **100**

Now try this!
4 = 1 × 4, 2 × 2
6 = 1 × 6, 2 × 3
8 = 1 × 8, 2 × 4
9 = 1 × 9, 3 × 3
10 = 1 × 10, 2 × 5
12 = 2 × 6, 3 × 4
16 = 2 × 8, 4 × 4
18 = 2 × 9, 3 × 6
20 = 2 × 10, 4 × 5
24 = 3 × 8, 4 × 6
30 = 3 × 10, 5 × 6
36 = 4 × 9, 6 × 6
40 = 4 × 10, 5 × 8

p 32

The 16 divisions are:
12 ÷ 4 = 3   18 ÷ 6 = 3   14 ÷ 7 = 2
21 ÷ 7 = 3   28 ÷ 7 = 4   42 ÷ 7 = 6
16 ÷ 8 = 2   24 ÷ 8 = 3   32 ÷ 8 = 4
56 ÷ 8 = 7   18 ÷ 9 = 2   27 ÷ 9 = 3
36 ÷ 9 = 4   54 ÷ 9 = 6   63 ÷ 9 = 7
72 ÷ 9 = 8

Now try this!
Examples include: 36 ÷ 2 = 18, 48 ÷ 3 = 16

p 33

p 34

1. 52   **2.** 2   **3.** 19
4. 5   **5.** 0   **6.** 8
7. 6   **8.** 10   **9.** 4

p 35

1. 1600 cm²   **2.** 4900 cm²   **3.** 2500 cm²
4. 3600 cm²   **5.** 6400 cm²
6. 8100 cm²   **7.** 10 000 cm²

Now try this!
£250   £40   £160

p 36

1. 0·43 m   **2.** 0·57 m   **3.** 0·39 m   **4.** 0·94 m   **5.** 0·29 m
6. 0·76 m   **7.** 0·86 m   **8.** 0·67 m   **9.** 0·72 m
10. 1·84 m   **11.** 1·36 m   **12.** 0·52 m   **13.** 1·08 m
14. 1·64 m   **15.** 1·56 m

Now try this!
0·48 m   0·39 m

p 38

1. 370   **2.** 490   **3.** 730
4. 830   **5.** 560   **6.** 920
7. 660   **8.** 980   **9.** 760
10. 1680   **11.** 1520   **12.** 580
13. 1740   **14.** 980   **15.** 1560

Now try this!
1840   1480   760   960

Answers

p 39
1. b is correct, final winnings £9200
2. a is correct, final winnings £4200
3. a is correct, final winnings £3900
4. b is correct, final winnings £3650
5. c is correct, final winnings £17400
6. b is correct, final winnings £79 000
Now try this!
£51 200   £25

p 40
1. 30 × 9 = 270   2. 50 × 7 = 350
3. 70 × 8 = 560   4. 90 × 6 = 540
5. 50 × 9 = 450   6. 30 × 8 = 240
7. 110 × 6 = 660   8. 12 × 70 = 840
9. 9 × 90 = 810
Now try this!
400 cm²   330 cm²   630 cm²

p 41
1. 270   2. 405   3. 345
4. 240   5. 675   6. 510
7. 255   8. 360   9. 945
Now try this!
14 × 35 =490   21 × 35 = 735

p 42
1. £1400   2. £2150   3. £1950   4. £5600   5. £2700
6. £850   7. £1150   8. £425   9. £925   10. £1475
Now try this!
£350   £575   £1050

p 43
x 6   6, 12, 18, 24, 30, 36, 42, 48, 54, 60
x 12 12, 24, 36, 48, 60, 72, 84, 96, 108, 120
x 24 24, 48, 72, 96, 120, 144, 168, 192, 216, 240
x 7   7, 14, 21, 28, 35, 42, 49, 56, 63, 70
1. 126   2. 168   3. 70
4. 196   5. 84   6. 224
Now try this!
48   108
96   216

p 44
x 26   26, 52, 104, 208, 416
x 31   31, 62, 124, 248, 496
x 37   37, 74, 148, 296, 592
Pop concert: £444
               £888
               £407
Musical: £234
               £442
               £364
Panto: £155
               £217
               £868
Now try this!
26 × 26 = 676   31 × 31 = 961

p 45
1. 102   2. 64   3. 126
4. 57   5. 96   6. 65
7. 126   8. 119   9. 152
10. 128   11. 162   12. 133
Now try this!
13 × 12 = 156   17 × 12 = 204
11 × 12 = 132   19 × 12 = 228

p 46
1. 1313   2. 1818   3. 1616   4. 2323
5. 1386   6. 1188   7. 2079   8. 1881
Now try this!
2814   2786

p 47
1. 2341   2. 918   3. 1785   4. 1377
5. 1372   6. 784   7. 1911   8. 2058
Now try this!
58   106

p 48
1. b 322   2. c 304   3. a 513
4. a 356   5. c 408   6. b 592
Now try this!
z 522   x 602   y 608

p 49
1. 1·2 × 4   2. 4·7 × 2
3. 7·1 × 8   4. 8·2 × 4 **or** 4·1 × 8
5. 2·8 × 7   6. 7·4 × 8
7. 5·1 × 3   8. 6·3 × 5
9. 9·1 × 6   10. 6·5 × 9
11. 5·3 × 9   12. 1·9 × 6
Now try this!
2·4 × 6   4·8 × 3   3·6 × 4

p 50
1. 0·65   2. 9·94   3. 0·8   4. 2·6   5. 9·6
6. 12   7. 9·94   8. 7   9. 4   10. 8
11. 2·8   12. 0·65   13. 1·42   14. 0·8

p 51
1. 243   2. 56·3   3. 760
4. 840   5. 25   6. 376
7. 10   8. 10   9. 100
10. 100   11. 10   12. 10
13. 4·09   14. 2·78
Now try this!
£32·50   £47·80   £57·50   £64·90

p 52
1. 0·64   2. 0·73   3. 0·07   4. 0·09   5. 2·8
6. 6·4   7. 10   8. 100   9. 100   10. 10
11. 1   12. 6   13. 17   14. 93
Now try this!
0·03 m   0·17 m   0·24 m   0·25 m

p 54
1. 16 926   2. 7752   3. 31 925   4. 9888
5. 19 024   6. 26 082
Now try this!
4728 × 7 = 33 096

p 55
1. 8188   2. 13 237   3. 9316   4. 17 145
Now try this!
largest: 431 × 52 = 22 412

p 56
1. correct   2. correct   3. 13 745   4. 23 244   5. correct
6. 12 474   7. 24 624   8. correct   9. 15 308   10. correct

p 57
1. 12 972   2. 11 310   3. 13 992
4. 24 472   5. 10 620   6. 14 592
Now try this!
Various answers, for example: 235 × 46 = 10 810
                                   536 × 42 = 22 512
                                   632 × 45 = 28 440

p 58
a 14·76   b 22·12   c 16·35
d 19·72   e 15·48   f 11·52

actual order	f	a	e	c	d	b

Now try this!
Actual difference is 5·04

p 59
1. 24   2. 27   3. 33
4. 23   5. 26   6. 42
Now try this!
The answers match the number per team.

p 60
The divisions are all correct.